Implications of the Gospel

Implications of the Gospel

Lutheran-Episcopal Dialogue, Series III

Edited by
William A. Norgren and William G. Rusch
With a Study Guide by
Darlis J. Swan and Elizabeth Z. Turner

Augsburg • Minneapolis
Forward Movement Publications • Cincinnati

IMPLICATIONS OF THE GOSPEL
Lutheran–Episcopal Dialogue, Series III

This book is the Final Report of the Lutheran–Episcopal Dialogue, Series III (1983–1988) held under the auspices of the Episcopal Church, U.S.A., the Evangelical Lutheran Church in America, and the Lutheran Church–Missouri Synod.

Copyright © 1988 Augsburg Fortress

Published by Augsburg Fortress, 426 S. Fifth St., Box 1209, Minneapolis MN 55440 and Forward Movement Publications, 412 Sycamore St., Cincinnati OH 45202.

Scripture quotations unless otherwise noted are from the Revised Standard Version of the Bible, copyright 1946, 1952, and 1971 by the Division of Christian Education of the National Council of Churches.

Library of Congress Cataloging-in-Publication Data

Lutheran–Episcopal Dialogue (3rd series;
   1983–   )
   IMPLICATIONS OF THE GOSPEL.
   1. Evangelical Lutheran Church in America
—Relations—Episcopal Church.   2. Episcopal
Church—Relations—Evangelical Lutheran Church
in America.   3. Theology, Doctrinal.
4. Lutheran Church—Doctrines.   5. Episcopal
Church—Doctrines.   6. Anglican Communion
—Doctrines.   7. Anglican Communion—Relations
—Lutheran Church.   8. Lutheran Church—
Relations—Anglican Communion.   I. Norgren,
William A.   II. Rusch, William G.   III. Title.

BX5928.5.E95L88   1983   284.1'332   88-7729
ISBN 0-8066-2408-6

Manufactured in the U.S.A.   AF 10-2408

1   2   3   4   5   6   7   8   9   0   1   2   3   4   5   6   7   8   9

Contents

Study Guide for *Implications of the Gospel*

Implications
of the
Gospel

Preface

Episcopalians and Lutherans have been in dialogue on an international and national level for more than two decades. In 1982, the Episcopal Church in the U.S.A. and the three predecessors of the Evangelical Lutheran Church in America affirmed the progress of the dialogue to that date and declared the goal of their efforts was full communion. These affirmations and commitments were repeated by the Evangelical Lutheran Church in America at the time of its formation in 1988.

The churches declared in 1982 that on their way to full communion certain things needed to be accomplished. Among them, the need for continuing dialogue to deal with two main issues was identified. The Episcopalians wanted greater agreement on the ordering of the church as the community of apostolic faith. The Lutherans sought greater clarity on the claim that there was sufficient agreement on the gospel to enter into eucharistic fellowship. Both reactions were understandable. The churches had reached sufficient consensus to take a major step on the ecumenical journey and to enter into the Lutheran–Episcopal Agreement with Interim Sharing of the Eucharist. Now greater consensus on important aspects of the Christian faith and community was requested so that the churches could take the next steps.

As a result of the Agreement of 1982, a third series of dialogues was initiated by the churches. It took up its work in 1983 and began by concentrating on the first part of the mandate given to it by the churches: the *Implications of the Gospel*. After four years of work the Lutheran–Episcopal Dialogue, Series III, completed its work on this topic. The following pages contain the dialogue's report on the first half of the 1982 request. The dialogue is continuing work on the second half of the mandate.

Implications of the Gospel will appear to many readers to be a different type of dialogue report from most. Conspicuously, it is longer. It addresses many topics in language somewhat unfamiliar to both traditions. Many of the points that have not been divisive between Lutherans and Episcopalians are discussed extensively. Perhaps the greatest contributions of the document are two: (1) it reveals how much these two different traditions with their own histories are able to say together; (2) it challenges the churches to develop new levels of trust, cooperation, and mission.

If the churches are able to accept the challenge contained in *Implications of the Gospel,* they will be moving further along the path toward full communion.

Thus the stage has been reached where the dialogue has completed part of its work and transmitted it to the churches. The churches individually and together must seriously weigh and consider this document. They must determine the degree to which they can accept the recommendations and change their thinking and practices.

On behalf of the dialogue representatives, we commend their work to the churches for their prayerful and serious consideration. It is our prayer that this document may provide one of the means to enable the churches under God's Spirit to move toward the greater unity we believe God wills for Christ's people.

William A. Norgren
The Ecumenical Officer, Episcopal Church in the United States of America.

William G. Rusch
Executive Director, Office for Ecumenical Affairs, the Evangelical Lutheran Church in America.

Introduction

1. In September 1982, four American churches took an official action of historical importance. The Episcopal Church in the U.S.A. and three Lutheran churches, the American Lutheran Church, the Association of Evangelical Lutheran Churches, and the Lutheran Church of America, approved an agreement which contains the following provisions:

1. The churches "welcome and rejoice in the substantial progress of the Lutheran–Episcopal Dialogues (LED) I and II and the Anglican–Lutheran International Conversations."

2. The churches recognize each other as churches "in which the Gospel is preached and taught."

3. The churches "encourage the development of common Christian life throughout the respective churches by such means as the following:

   a. Mutual prayer and mutual support, including parochial/congregational and diocesan/synodical covenants or agreements;

   b. Common study of the Holy Scriptures, the historical and theological traditions of each church, and the materials of LED I and II;

   c. Joint programs of religious education, theological discussion, mission, evangelism and social action;

   d. Joint use of physical facilities."

4. The churches "affirm now on the basis of studies of LED I and LED II and of the Anglican–Lutheran International Conversations that the basic teaching of each respective church is consonant with the Gospel and is sufficiently compatible with the teaching of" the other churches "that a relationship

of Interim Sharing of the Eucharist is hereby established between these churches in the U(nited) S(tates of) A(merica)."

5. The churches "authorize and establish now a third series of Lutheran–Episcopal Dialogues for the discussion of any other outstanding questions that must be resolved before full communion (*communio in sacris*/altar and pulpit fellowship) can be established between the respective churches, e.g., *Implications of the Gospel,* historic episcopate, and ordering of ministry (bishops, priests, and deacons) in the total context of apostolicity" (emphasis added).

2. The four churches mentioned above have been joined in the third series of dialogues by the Lutheran Church–Missouri Synod, which participated in LED I and LED II but did not join in the Agreement of 1982. The assignment being fulfilled by this report is that the participants of LED III address the topic "Implications of the Gospel" as one of the "outstanding questions that must be resolved before full communion can be established between the respective churches." In the fulfillment of the assignment the participants have been encouraged and informed by the work done in the previous Lutheran–Episcopal Dialogues (LED I, pp. 13-33, LED II, pp. 22-53) as well as the work of Episcopal and Lutheran bilateral conversations with the Roman Catholic and Reformed traditions.

3. As the 1972 Pullach Report of the International Anglican–Lutheran Conversations noted, Lutherans and Episcopalians "have in the past lived largely in separation and in relative isolation from one another" despite "occasional contacts and a common awareness of great areas of affinity of doctrine, worship, and church life" (LED II, p. 137). Whether the isolation or the affinity has been more responsible, the fact remains that there have been no divisive theological controversies between the two churches. As a consequence, our attention to

the topic, "Implications of the Gospel," was not directed toward the task of overcoming doctrinal differences, clearing away entrenched prejudices, reconciling conflicting liturgical practices, or lifting historic condemnations.

4. Given these historical circumstances, we have taken it as our task in the present document to utilize the vision articulated by converging theological scholarship in both of our churches. With the help of this vision, we have tried to listen afresh to the Holy Scriptures as the "rule and ultimate standard" *(Book of Common Prayer,* p. 877), or "the authoritative source and norm" (Constitution of the Evangelical Lutheran Church in America, 2.03, p. 13) of our common Christianity, to discover common insights in the creeds we both confess, and to draw upon the renewal of our shared liturgical heritage. We wish to show what Episcopalians and Lutherans can say about implications of the gospel as an indication of our growing consensus. If we have not always used traditional terms, phrases, and formulations in what follows, that does not mean neglect of or disdain for our traditions. It means rather that we have been drawn through our traditions to a statement of the gospel grounded in the death and resurrection of Jesus which calls us to live by faith in the promise of the reign of God and its ultimate consummation. Our approach in this document has an apologetic character. Our intention is to address the contemporary situation out of our two traditions. If we want to talk about the gospel together, we need to ask and respond to two fundamental sets of questions:

(1) How shall we say the gospel today? What is the present truth of the gospel? How can the gospel be communicated intelligibly in a contemporary culture?

(2) Is a contemporary saying of the gospel faithful? How does our present saying of the gospel reflect what we have learned from the pre-Enlightenment theological traditions of the church? Above all, how is our saying of the gospel faithful

to the norm of Christianity, the Scriptures of the Old and New Testaments?

One way to respond to both questions is to say the gospel in terms of what God is doing in history: the history of Israel and its expectations, the history of Jesus as the Christ, our history as the persons to whom and through whom the gospel is addressed, and ultimately the world's history and the outcome promised by the gospel. This approach is somewhat different from documents that have originated in other bilateral dialogues. Like all such documents, however, it is historically conditioned and provisional as we consider the life and mission of the church on the threshold of the 21st century.

5. A brief description of the structure of this document may facilitate its reading and appropriation. In Section 1 the document begins with Jesus' proclamation of the reign of God,[1] a proclamation like that of the prophet of the exile (Isa. 52:7) who announced the good news of the reign of God in the midst of Judah's defeat, destruction, and exile. What makes the proclamation of Jesus more than an unfounded hope is the resurrection. The disciple community's encounters with Jesus after his resurrection enabled it to reenvision God's future, a future not yet consummated but already present as promise, and to reappropriate the past, Jesus' past life, ministry, and crucifixion as well as Israel's past. Because the death and resurrection of Jesus is the grounding of the promise, baptism is the way Christians are identified with Jesus and become witnesses to the promise. The crucifixion of Jesus defines the character of God's redeeming love and encourages the disciple community in the midst of costly and persecuted witness.

Section 2 takes up the great doctrines of classical Christianity, the doctrine of Christ and the doctrine of the Trinity, and identifies them as doctrines of the gospel. The Christian understanding of God is profoundly *evangelical,* that is, gospel-oriented. Faith in God is not faith in the irrational or unseen, but it is rather faith in the gospel.

Section 3 deals with the church as necessary implication of the gospel in terms of its liturgy, polity, and doctrine. Because the church is the continuation of the mission of Jesus, it must be conscious of its origins in Israel and the implications of its origins for its continuing relationship with Judaism.

Section 4 seeks to understand the world addressed by the gospel as well as the implications of the gospel for key dimensions of the life of the world.

Section 5 takes up the mission of the gospel in the world in terms of the church's call to be one, to witness to the gospel, and to live out its calling.

I. The Eschatological *Grounding* of the Gospel

A. The Proclamation and Ministry of Jesus

6. When Jesus came preaching the gospel of God, he said, according to the Gospel of Mark, "The time is fulfilled, and the kingdom of God is at hand; repent, and believe in the gospel" (Mark 1:15). In the Lukan account Jesus begins his mission by reading in the synagogue a programmatic promise from the scroll of the prophet Isaiah and then announcing to the assembly, "Today this scripture has been fulfilled in your hearing" (Luke 4:17-21). The Gospels of the New Testament proclaim that the good news (gospel) is the advent in history of the redemptive reign of God. Jesus begins the consummation and realization of the great vision of Israel's prophet of the exile: "Your God reigns" (Isa. 52:7; cf. 61:1-2).

7. The documents of the New Testament use a variety of phrases, images, and concepts to give expression to the gospel. Paul, whose letters are among the earliest documents in the New Testament, proclaimed the gospel in terms of persons being "justified by faith in Christ, and not by works of the law" (Gal. 2:16). Paul condemned anything but "the grace of Christ" as a different gospel, no gospel at all, a perversion of the gospel (Gal. 1:6-7). Jesus is the justifier as the crucified one (Gal. 2:20-21). The Gospel of John, among the later documents in the New Testament, proclaimed the gospel as the eternal Word of God become flesh, dwelling among us, revealing grace, truth, and God (John 1:1-18). The "hour" for which he had come, and through which the "glory" of the

Father and the Son would be revealed, and on the basis of which the Paraclete would be bestowed, was the cross, resurrection, and ascension of Jesus (John 14–17). The synoptic Gospels—Matthew, Mark, and Luke—although each is written from a unique perspective, proclaimed the mission and ministry of Jesus in terms of the breaking in of the reign of God. It is important to note that the central emphasis of the Gospel of Mark is to understand that the breaking in of the reign of God took place through the cross (Mark 8:27-35; 9:30-32; 10:32-45).

8. What identifies the proclamation of the cross as *good* news is the "eschatological" way of thinking in the New Testament. The writings of the New Testament are strongly focused in a future hope. That future hope is expressed by the theological term *eschaton* from which the word "eschatology" is derived. In traditional theological thought "eschatology" dealt with "last things," what would take place when history had come to an end. We are using the term "eschatology" in a closely related but nevertheless distinct sense, namely, as referring to the "outcome" of history, the ultimate goal or destiny or future toward which God is directing the history of the world. This "outcome" is present to us as the *promise* of the final victory of the reign of God. Most of the writings of the New Testament proclaim that in Christ the new age, the "eschatological age," has already begun, that the new age is now in tension with the ongoing "old age." The New Testament writings proclaim that the presence of the reign of God was already disclosed in the deeds, the teaching, and above all the death and resurrection of Jesus, the Christ.

B. The Significance of the Resurrection of Jesus

9. The decisive event for opening Jesus' disciples to this conviction was the resurrection of Jesus. After his execution and

burial the disciples were demoralized, defeated. The Gospel of Luke describes the two disciples on the way to Emmaus as assuming that Jesus had been discredited as Messiah by his crucifixion (Luke 24:21). What changed the disciples was their encounter with Jesus after his death. What they experienced was not a resuscitation, not their teacher resuming his life with them. Rather, Jesus encountered them now as the disclosure of the *eschaton* (outcome) proleptically, that is, in preview. Jesus encountered them as the beginning of the final hoped-for reign of God. The concepts available to them for describing what had happened to Jesus came from the eschatological expectations of Israel: that righteous sufferers would be vindicated, martyrs would be resuscitated (2 Maccabees 7:9-23). But the character of their encounters with Jesus after his death burst the framework of those expectations. They encountered someone and something radically *more,* not less, than those expectations. They experienced proleptically, that is, in preview, the outcome of history in the midst of history. They were let in on the disclosed promise of God's final salvation. The conviction of the earliest disciples eventually found expression in a variety of related convictions, implications of the gospel in the various documents of the New Testament. There would be "no condemnation" for those joined to the Christ (Rom. 8:1). The power of death was not to have the last word (1 Cor. 15:54-57). The fallen (old) age and its powers had been subjected to the Christ (Eph. 1:15-23, especially vv. 21-23). The "world" as hostile to God's reign had been overcome (John 16:33). All tears would be wiped away (Rev. 7:13-17; cf. Isa. 25:6-8).

10. In their encounter with the resurrection of Jesus, the disciples at last understood something of the paradox that the crucified one was and is, despite all appearances, God's "Yes" to the world (2 Cor. 1:18-24). The good news which Jesus announced had indeed been an act as well as a teaching of

grace, of unconditional promise (Luke 4:17-21; cf. Isa. 61:1-2). The resurrection disclosed that sin and death could not inhibit his freedom to be for the world or qualify his commitment to his creation (Rom. 8:18-39). The disclosure that the final consummation of history would be the reign of God meant the reaffirmation of the goodness of creation as well as effecting the reconciliation of an estranged humanity. The one who is Lord and Christ is also the one through whom "all things were created," in whom "all things hold together" (John 1:1-5; Col. 1:15-20).

11. The church confessed the death and resurrection of Jesus as good news for the world by rejecting the gnostic attempt to drive a wedge between creation and redemption. The following were among the ways the church affirmed the creation: the acknowledgment of the Scriptures of Israel as canonical Scriptures for the church; the continuity with Israel and its worship traditions (Psalter, Blessings, Thanksgivings); the creedal affirmation that the God of creation is identical with Jesus, his Father, and the Holy Spirit; the principle of sacramentality (that the creaturely is capable of being the vehicle for God's ultimate promise); and the expectation of the resurrection of all because the risen Jesus was the "first fruits." All of this testified to the conviction that the gospel as eschatological event was not a repudiation of the world but its fulfillment and hope.

C. Baptism and the Eschatological Age

12. Baptism into the death and resurrection of Jesus was practiced by the earliest disciples on the basis of the resurrection of Jesus. It was both similar to and different from the baptizing of John the Baptist. John's was a baptism of *repentance* in anticipation of the coming reign of God. The baptism practiced by Jesus' disciples in his name recognizes that the reign of

God is both "now" and "yet to be consummated." This comes to expression in two ways.

13. First, baptism in the name of Jesus or in the triune name is both *initiation* into the community of the *eschaton* already present in Jesus by means of being identified with Jesus' death and resurrection, and it is also *repentance* in anticipation of the final realization of the promise of Jesus. The baptized are grasped by the forgiving love of God, transferred to the kingdom of his beloved Son, in whom we have redemption, the forgiveness of sins (cf. Col. 1:13-14). Although repentance and faith often precede baptism, its character as initiation through identification with the death and resurrection of Jesus means that something happens *to* the candidate. This then becomes one reason for the baptism of infants. Because they share in the fallenness of humanity, their baptism is necessary. However, they also share in the present promise of the reign of God (Mark 10:14-16 and parallels; Matt. 18:3). Because the consummation of the reign of God is still awaited, candidates can also be summoned to "repent and be baptized" (e.g., Acts 2:38). Indeed, all who have been initiated into the eschatological community are called to repent in view of their still flawed and broken witness to the reign of God. Because they *have* died with Christ (Col. 2:20-23), they can be exhorted to "put to death" what is sinful (that is, whatever resists the reign of God), to "put away" whatever is characteristic of the "old nature" (Col. 3:5-11). Because they have been raised with Christ (Col. 3:1-4), they are exhorted to be clothed with all that is characteristic of the new nature (Col. 3:12-17).

14. Second, because the reign of God is both "now" and "yet to be consummated," the present existence of the eschatological community is characterized by temptation, that is, by assault on its identity, by struggle and conflict, by brokenness and lapses into unfaithfulness. Baptism is thus initiation into

the *locus* of conflict between the old age and the new (Eph. 6:10-20). Because of baptism we can recognize that we are, in Martin Luther's phrase, simultaneously righteous and sinful. Baptism means that while we are grasped by the grace and power of the Holy Spirit, that is, by the gift and power of God's freedom for the future, we experience at the same time the continued power of the demonic. Hence baptism is the sacrament *par excellence* of justification *by faith*[2] for it initiates into a community which lives in the "land of promise" and which anticipates the city "whose builder and maker is God" (Heb. 11:10). Baptism plunges us into the situation in which the "old" (that is, the power of all that is hostile to the reign of God) has passed away (2 Cor. 5:17), but is still able to afflict, perplex, persecute, or strike down (2 Cor. 4:7-18).

15. Thus in the Lutheran rite of baptism those who are "set free from the bondage to sin and death" by being baptismally joined "to the death and resurrection of our Lord Jesus Christ" are asked to "renounce all the forces of evil, the devil, and all his empty promises" (*The Lutheran Book of Worship*, pp. 121-125). In the Episcopal rite of baptism those who are led by the Christ, "through his death and resurrection, from the bondage of sin into everlasting life" are asked to renounce "Satan and all the spiritual forces of wickedness that rebel against God. . . . the evil powers of this world which corrupt and destroy the creature of God. . . . the sinful desires that draw [us] from the love of God" (*The Book of Common Prayer*, pp. 301-308). Both liturgical traditions testify to the conviction that baptism links us with the death and resurrection of Jesus and therefore calls us to the struggle against evil and its power in ourselves and in the world.

D. The Bondage of Sin

16. The "old aeon" from which we are delivered by God's eschatological salvation is characterized by our bondage to the

power of sin and death, by our perversion of God's call to be creatures both finite and free, by our alienation from the image of God given with our creation. Our fallenness is disclosed when we deny either our finitude or our freedom or both; or when we refuse to be creatures or to be accountable or both; or when we use our best behaviors, insights, and achievements as occasions for idolatry or as a means of self-justification; or when we despair of God's mercy and engage in self-hatred. Our sin, in other words, is the bondage of misdirected trust, false faith. One sign of judgment upon such sin is that we are handed over to our idols. Captive to the powers of the fallen aeon, we reveal our bondage through attempts at exclusivistic self-preservation and self-protection, through our denial of the truth or our despair of God's mercy, or through our adherence to power and privilege at the expense of authentic peace and universal justice. This is the bondage from which the redemptive reign of God sets us free and at the same time the bondage which continues to assault and, at times, overwhelm the baptized.

E. The Gospel as the Word and Way of the Cross

17. The resurrection is God's act of proclaiming that the "Christ" title is now qualified by, determined by, the cross (Acts 2:36; Rom. 1:4). Jesus the crucified one is the Christ (1 Cor. 2:2). This proclamation calls into question every attempt of the church to pervert the gospel of God's reign into false "glory" or triumphalism. The word of the cross is the weapon given to the church in its struggle with various temptations, e.g., the temptation to substitute psychological manipulation, religious loyalty, or political and military power for the gospel.

18. The cross of Jesus defines the reign of God as an act of redeeming, sin-bearing suffering and death. Jesus incarnates the sovereign choice to be a victim so that others need not be

victimized. The reign of God is the reign of the one who consents to suffer in and with and for the world. The vision of such a God was given to Israel (e.g., Hos. 11:8-9; Jer. 31:18-20) and came to fulfillment when the Messiah of God was proclaimed as identical with the suffering servant of God. (Mark 1:11 and its parallels make a direct link between a messianic enthronement song, Psalm 2, and the Servant Song, Isa. 42:1-4.) God's reign is therefore proclaimed as the reign of one who enters into solidarity with slaves and who dies the humiliating death of a slave (Phil. 2:5-11). It is the reign of the despised and crucified one (1 Cor. 1:18—2:5; 1 Peter 2:21-25; Heb. 13:12-16; Mark 10:35-45 and parallels), whose crucifixion is also his exaltation (John 3:14; 8:28; and 12:31-32). It is the reign of the abandoned one in whose death the Father and the Son experience the depths of condemnation and alienation and thus open the human future anew to the Spirit of creative love (Romans 8, esp. vv. 31-39; Gal. 3:13). It is the reign of "the Lamb of God, who takes away the sin of the world" (John 1:29). The cross of Jesus establishes God's redemptive reign. It is also the concrete way in which it engages in continued conflict with the powers of the "old aeon," that is, the powers of sin and death.

II. The *God* of the Gospel

A. The History of Jesus and the Christological Dogma

19. The God of the church's confession, Father, Son, Holy Spirit, is the God of the gospel. The church is continuously led to that confession by the gospel and its implications. The church's path to its confession of God was historical in content: the history of Israel and the history of Jesus. The Scriptures of Israel grew out of Israel's history, where God is portrayed as one who calls, elects, and covenants with a people, who creates and redeems, who rules and judges the nations and the cosmos, who gives Torah and sends the prophets, whose very character is expressed in vulnerability and the determination to suffer with, for, at the hands of the world, whose involvement in history is directed toward such ends as peace (shalom), justice (righteousness), and wholeness (life).

20. Jesus of Nazareth appears in Israel's history as eschatological prophet with both implicit and explicit messianic claims. His enemies intended his crucifixion as judgment upon his claim to be the Christ of God, the one calling Israel to its mission on behalf of the reign of God. The crucifixion was intended as a rejection of the words and deeds by which Jesus proclaimed the reign of God and embodied its power. But the gospel declares that he is indeed the Christ, so designated by the resurrection (Rom. 1:3-4; Acts 2:36). The resurrection points the church both forward toward the consummation of the redemptive reign of God and simultaneously directs attention back to the cross and its significance in the light of the entire ministry of Jesus.

21. In the wake of the resurrection encounters with Jesus, the community of his disciples moved through and beyond the recognition that he was inaugurating the reign of God to the confession that he and his history are to be regarded as one with God. In the words of an early Christian author (2 Clement 1:1), "we ought to think of Jesus Christ as we do of God." The history of Jesus, his ministry, cross, and resurrection, con firms, renews, and transforms Israel's experience and confession. That same history of Jesus is the basis for the church's trinitarian and christological dogmas. What the church *means evangelically* by confessing that Jesus has a divine nature is not that assumptions from philosophy about the qualities of deity (e.g., that the divine is "infinite" or "immortal" or "omnipotent") are applied to the historical Jesus. Rather, the evangelical meaning is that the historical person, Jesus, weak and crucified, is what we mean when we speak of God as redeemer (Col. 1:15-20). In his ministry the call to Israel to serve the reign of God comes to final and definitive expression. In his death God suffers with, for, or at the hands of his people and their enemies. In his resurrection the promise of the final triumph of God's reign is proleptically present.

22. There are three reasons why the way of thinking described above (pars. 19-21) is of decisive importance for our understanding of the gospel.

First, it serves the intelligibility of the church's witness. It must be noted that making the gospel understood does not make it easier to believe. Rather it makes evident the genuine alternatives with which humanity is confronted. It discloses that our predicament is not ignorance of the gospel but sinful trust in false gospels. The church's recovery of the *historical* character of its gospel makes its proclamation more apparent to contemporary culture. The meaning of God in terms of ultimacy and of the gospel in terms of historical finality is both more faithful and more meaningful. Thus the historical meaning of the "two natures" dogma of Chalcedon witnesses to the ultimate and final redemptive quality of Jesus' death and resurrection.

23. Second, the history of Jesus is the grounding of the grace of God both in the world's history and in God's history. It is the grounding of grace within the world's history because in the cross of Jesus God has made a final and unconditional commitment to the world. It is the grounding of grace within God's history because in the death and resurrection of Jesus something has happened to God that had not happened before. God's vulnerability and suffering was known in Israel (e.g., Hosea, Jeremiah). In Jesus that vulnerability and suffering receives its final expression, namely death itself. In Jesus God experiences the depth of sin (2 Cor. 5:21) and the power of death (Rom. 5:8). Thus sin and death have been encountered and overcome in the being and history of God. With sin overcome and death behind him, Jesus can and does make an unconditional promise to the world: the triumph of the reign of God will finally be manifested.

24. Third, the cross as central to the history of Jesus gives Christianity an absolute or unconditional gospel which is not imperialistic, immoral, or triumphalistic. Religion by definition is about absolutes. The tragic character of inauthentic or false absolutes is that they establish themselves through destructive power, the forced imposition of that which is alien. The reaction to such imposition is the equally inappropriate and false assertion of autonomy. The absolute of the historical Jesus means the proclamation of a gospel in which God reconciles the world by means of the absolute quality of suffering servanthood (2 Cor. 5:17-21; John 12:31-32; Phil. 2:5-11; Eph. 2:13-22). The church commends its gospel with a servant ministry grounded in the person and history of Jesus (2 Cor. 6:1-10).

B. The Trinity and the Gospel

25. The church's name of God, "Father, Son, Holy Spirit," is grounded in Jesus Christ. Among other things, *name* implies narrative, the story of the one being named. Because the gospel is the historical narrative of God's commitment to the world, God's determination to create and redeem the world, and finally God's victorious promise of an unconquerable future for the world, the church told the story of God in terms of the triune name. The trinity is the way the church identifies and confesses God because of Jesus, because of the gospel.

26. Jesus is identified as "Son," sent by one whom he called "Abba," an intimate term for "Father." He invited his disciples to use the name "Father" when he taught them to pray the mission prayer of the present and promised reign of God. Both names, "Father" and "Son," reflect and express the gospel as the love of God for the world and the love within the triune God. As we have learned in the self-giving love of Jesus, the Son, God's love never turns in on itself. It is forever directed toward another. The act of creating, of calling into existence a universe distinct from God, is expressive of the love which is God. The act of reconciling a fallen humanity is consistent with a loving creator. Suffering will be the loss of both creator and reconciler. Both the Son and the Father suffer, each in his own way, in the cross.

27. The Son "gave himself for [us]" (Gal. 2:20) in a profound unity of will with his Father, who "gave him up for us all" (Rom. 8:32). When the Son's cry from the cross reveals his entry into forsakenness (Mark 15:34) and condemnation (Gal. 3:13), it occurs under the darkness of his Father's hidden face (Mark 15:33). The death that is experienced goes to the very heart of God's being. The Son sacrificed his relationship to his Father, and his Father sacrificed his relationship to his Son.

"God *so* loved the world that he gave his only Son" (John 3:16, italics added). That is, God loved the world *in this way,* the way of forsakenness in Jesus' death on the cross.

28. The farewell words of Jesus in the Gospel of John speak of the Holy Spirit as the one who "stands alongside of" (*paracletos,* John 14:16, 26; 15:26; 16:7) the persecuted community in its life in the world (John 15:18-25). In this role the Spirit of truth (John 14:17; 15:26; 16:13) continues to bear the witness of Jesus in the world concerning sin, righteousness, and judgment (John 16:8), and guides the community into the truth of Jesus' revelation of the Father (John 16:12-15). In the power of the Spirit the community is sent into the world by the risen Lord (John 20:17-18, 21-23). Through the Holy Spirit the suffering Son and Father are thus united with the condemned and cursed, with helpless victims and helpless participants in the suffering of victims, finally even with oppressors in the overcoming of their sin. It is thus critical in the present missionary context of the church to understand that the proclamation of the suffering God aids mission. In terms of post-Holocaust Europe, this statement will be evident enough. In the case of middle-class America, much suffering is psychological and veiled, and it will therefore have to be exposed and named as "suffering." Then the liberating message of the suffering God will be at hand, and will be the tool for mission in our context of suffering. Because God is *Emmanu-el,* God with us, there is now hope for the hopeless, forgiveness for sinners, comfort for the forsaken, vision for the victims, resurrection for the dead. In Christ God's holiness, that is, God's otherness and uniqueness, is not condemning and threatening. God's holiness is God's own and unique compassion. Paul expresses to the Galatian Christians that it is through the Spirit that faith has come in the hearing of the gospel (Gal. 3:2), in which the hearer receives God's promise of inheritance in Jesus: "God has sent the Spirit of his Son into our hearts, crying, 'Abba!

Father!' " (Gal. 4:6). Being led by the Spirit is walking in the Spirit, putting to death the old enslavements, and living in the freedom of Christ to love and serve the neighbor (Gal. 5:1— 6:6). The Ephesian letter takes up this theme by stating that the Holy Spirit represents the down payment (Eph. 1:13-14) which enables us to live in our inheritance "until we acquire possession of it." The dynamic of a new future is open to the world. The Holy Spirit is the power (*dynamis*) of that new and reconciled future. The trinity is the God of the gospel. The name of God, Father, Son, Holy Spirit, reflects the historical particularity of the gospel itself.

29. Our churches need to be concerned about the overuse of the term "Father," especially in the address of God in prayer. When the term Father is not clearly used as part of the trinitarian name of God (cf. par. 31 below), it functions instead as a masculine image for God. While we recognize that the church has traditionally selected masculine images for God from the Scriptures, our churches need to advocate the use of feminine images as well as this traditional masculine imagery. We need all the imagery available to help us think about God. When the term Father is used as an image, as an analogy drawn from our experience, it must be supplemented by many other images and analogies in order to reflect the fullness of our experiences. Such supplementing will, of course, include feminine imagery. Especially in prayer, when it is appropriate to add modifying clauses in the address of God, the use of feminine imagery needs to be encouraged. (Examples: O God, whose love for us is like that of a mother, who suffers for us as woman in giving birth, who would gather us as mother hen gathers her chicks, etc.) There is ample precedent for such imagery in the Bible and the rest of the church's tradition (Deut. 32:18; Job 38:28-29; Ps. 123:2; Isa. 42:14; Hos. 13:8; Matt. 23:37; and Luke 13:34).[3] Strategies for introducing the feminine element into talk about God do not stop with the first Person of the

Trinity. Scholars have recovered the biblical theme of Jesus as the "Sophia" of God. Others find feminine symbols to be appropriately descriptive of the Spirit's work. (The words for "spirit" vary in grammatical as distinct from sexual gender from language to language, being feminine in Hebrew and Aramaic, neuter in Greek, and masculine in Latin.)

30. We are aware that others advocate the substitution of gender-neutral terms, such as "creator," "redeemer," "sanctifier," for the trinitarian name. This reaction is understandable both because of the centuries of patriarchalism in the church and because, when the dogma of the trinity has been separated from the gospel and has instead been understood as a component of Christian ideology, it has been used in an oppressive manner. However the church *cannot* simply substitute the designations creator, redeemer, and sanctifier for the trinitarian name. We cannot do so because function is *not* identical with person and because each function is ascribed to all three persons encompassed by the one trinitarian name.

31. Furthermore, since the dogma of the trinity is a confession and naming of the God of the gospel, "Father" is not, on the one hand, just one image among other biblical images, nor, on the other hand, does it exhaust the church's name for God. It is the name by which Jesus addressed the one in whose mission and history he participates. Hence the church's full dogmatic name for God is "Father, Son, Holy Spirit." When we address the "Abba" of Jesus, we do so because we have been called to participate in the liberating mission of the gospel by the Father, Son, Holy Spirit.

> For you did not receive the spirit of slavery to fall back into fear, but you have received the spirit of sonship. When we cry, "Abba! Father!" it is the Spirit himself bearing witness with our spirit that we are children of God, and if children, then

heirs, heirs of God and fellow heirs with Christ, provided we suffer with him in order that we may also be glorified with him.

(Rom. 8:15-17)

To abandon the "Abba" name given us by Jesus is to diminish the liberating mission of the gospel.

32. The uniqueness and finality of the God of the gospel must be confessed in such a way as to be grounded in the particular history of Jesus. God is *one* because the meaning of God's oneness is God's uniqueness, singularity, finality, ultimacy. The gospel defines and identifies that uniqueness, that singularity, that finality, that ultimacy. The gospel is the history of the Son, his Father, and the promised Spirit in, with, and for the world, a history which points back to the being of God as eternal Trinity.

III. The *Church* of the Gospel

A. The Church as Necessary Implication of the Gospel

33. It is to be expected that the issues of greatest sensitivity related to full communion between Episcopalians and Lutherans would occur in ecclesiology. On the basis of Article 7 (VII) of the Augsburg Confession Lutherans have traditionally emphasized that the preaching of the gospel "in its purity" and the administration of the sacraments "according to the gospel" are "sufficient for the true unity of the Christian church." Lutherans have asked whether doctrine, proclamation, and administration of the sacraments reflect an authentic understanding of the gospel before entertaining the prospect of full communion with non-Lutheran churches. Anglicans have traditionally stressed the importance of order to assure the authentic administration of the sacraments. Episcopalians have asked, among other things, whether churches have the historic episcopate before entertaining the prospect of full communion with them.

34. In 1982, when the predecessor bodies of the Evangelical Lutheran Church in America and the Episcopal Church recognized each other as churches "in which the Gospel is preached and taught," this was done on the basis of official conversations both in Europe and the United States of America which revealed a significant shared understanding of the gospel of justification by grace for Christ's sake through faith (Anglican–Lutheran European Regional commission, 1983, pp. 8-10; Lutheran–Episcopal Dialogue II, 1981, pp. 22-25). The

agreement on the sacraments (ALERC, pp. 10-14; LED II, pp. 25-29) and on apostolicity (ALERC, pp. 14-20; LED II, pp. 31-43) was sufficient to permit both churches to take the historic step of establishing "Interim Sharing of the Eucharist" as they continued to work toward full communion. These agreements encourage us to affirm together what we understand about the church. It is our conviction that the gospel of the reign of God means that the church is called to be an eschatological community. This does not mean that the church is identical with the reign of God. Understanding the church as eschatological community, however, confirms the fresh approach to apostolicity begun by LED II and opens new possibilities for understanding questions of order envisioned when LED III was mandated.

35. To begin, we confess and affirm the necessary relationship between the gospel and the church. While God calls each of us by name and gives each of us personal faith, this confession and affirmation requires special attention in the American context because of the pervasive presence of religious individualism in that context. Because many of the European immigrants who came to the North American continent were seeking to escape the oppressive qualities of established churches, and because post–Enlightenment culture often identified Christianity with morality, it became relatively easy for persons to identify themselves as Christians without becoming part of the church. The revival practice of asking hearers simply to "accept Jesus as personal savior" coupled with the scarcity of clergy on the frontier contributed to the separation of gospel from church. Currently, much religious television encourages and reinforces the individualism endemic to our religious history.

36. We must describe the necessary relationship between gospel and church with some care. The common history of our

churches in the 16th century continues to remind us of the dangers of religious oppression, especially the insistence that *church* controls *gospel* or that the church believes something other than the gospel which calls it into being. We confess and affirm that church and gospel are necessarily related because both have to do with the reign of God. The gospel is grounded in the history of Jesus as the breaking in of the *end-time* reign of God. The goal and consequence of the mission of Jesus is nothing less than the renewed people of God now open to and called to include all peoples. Hence the church is the principal implication of the gospel in human history. The end-time reign of God implies and calls into being the end-time messianic community.

37. The mission of Jesus not only implies community. It requires community for its continuance. The church is called to be the explicit bearer of the gospel in history. There is no faith in Jesus, the Christ, as the grounding of the reign of God without the visible and audible proclamation of the gospel in word and sacraments. And there is no proclamation of the gospel in word and sacraments without a community and its ministry (Rom. 10:14-20). Word and sacraments are embedded and embodied in the end-time community and its life. The call of the gospel is not to individualized and isolated faith. It is the call that persons be translated from communities dominated by the reign of death to the community created and liberated by the Christ's reign of life. The authentic alternative to oppressive religious institutionalism is not religious individualism but rather a community shaped by the gospel of the Christ as the crucified one.

B. Israel as the Matrix of the Church

38. The church is rooted in the gospel of Jesus, the Christ, not because Jesus is the founder of a religious institution but because the church is the continuation of Jesus' mission to and

through Israel. Jesus' announcement of the presence of the reign of God recalled for Israel themes long present in its history, particularly its vocation to be a light to the nations (cf. Isa. 49:1-6; 60:1-7). Jesus' acts of healing are also to be seen in this context; they are effective signs (e.g., Luke 11:20; 17:21) pointing to the presence of the reign of God so that Israel may fulfill its calling. They are intended to make for reconciliation of oppositions and opponents, to include the excluded, to embody the vision of the gathering of all humanity (e.g., Matt. 15:21-28; Luke 7:1-10; 13:29-30).

39. Yet the life and mission of Jesus also embodies the calling of Israel as "a kingdom of priests and a holy nation" (Exod. 19:6) to stand over against the idolatries of the nations. Hence the presence and acts of Jesus stand forth as a sign of contradiction, a sign for deprecation by others (Luke 2:34; Luke 12:51-53; Matt. 10:34-36). Thus, whether for those with no investment or expectation beyond the things of this world (cf. Phil. 3:17-20), or conversely, for those who regard the world as worthless, Jesus and the signs are themselves a cause for division and contradiction. Even though the vision of the messianic age is the gathering of all nations to and in the one people of God, this would occur, according to the mission of Jesus, only through the costly renewal of Israel as a prelude to the call and conversion of the Gentiles.

40. Hence Jesus and these active signs of the reign of God, implications of his teaching, serve as symbols of a renewed Israel consecrated by sacrifice. Thus Jesus' teaching, his proclamation of the reign of God, and especially collections of his sayings such as the Sermon on the Mount, were addressed to Israel, or the circle of disciples which represented Israel. His commitment was to a renewal of Israel, never more so than at his final meal with the disciples before his passion. Jesus interpreted the meal in terms of his coming death as a pouring

out of his blood for the "many." This is not a turning away from Israel to the world beyond but precisely a turning toward that very Israel determined upon his death.[4] Yet the same act of final commitment to Israel is simultaneously one of final, eschatological opening to the Gentiles, that is, to the entirety of humanity beyond Israel in every time and place.

41. Finally, the proximity of the reign of God to and within human society was represented by Jesus in his calling and constituting of the Twelve from among his disciples as an eschatological act and sign. The Twelve are not called to establish the church as distinct from Israel. They are rather called to serve in microcosm as symbols of a renewed Israel. After the resurrection of Jesus the community of the disciples took steps to perpetuate the Twelve (Acts 1:15-27) and chose one to become with them "a witness to his resurrection," that is, one who could witness with them to the breaking in of the *eschaton*. That the Twelve become part of the eventual apostles underscores Israel's mission of being the focus for the gathering of the Gentiles into the end-time people of God. They serve an ultimately wider apostolicity as a sign to the people of God of its continuity with Israel, its matrix in Israel (Mark 3:13-19 and parallels; Luke 22:28-30).

42. In the messianic vision the people of God is to be "Israel plus Gentiles." That this vision exists today in broken form, with a *church* which confesses Jesus as the Christ and a *synagogue* which does not, has significant implications for the church's proclamation of the good news that Jesus is indeed the Christ. It means, first, that the final consummation of the *eschaton* is still ahead of us. It means, second, that Christians cannot claim that God has abandoned the Jews (cf. Romans 9–11, especially 9:4-5 and 11:25-36). It means, third, that for us "new covenant" or "New Testament" does not mean replacing God's covenant with Israel but means rather the beginning of renewed or consummated covenant. It means,

fourth, that we *churches* stand under a special call to offer love, care, commitment, and solidarity to *synagogue*. This is needed to overcome long centuries of oppression and persecution which have poisoned the relationship between church and synagogue and challenged the credibility of the church's confession that Jesus is the Christ, that the *eschaton* has begun. It means, finally, that together church and synagogue witness to humanity's flawed and broken capacity to be the bearer of the messianic vision and that we view our present ecclesial existence with appropriate modesty, humility, and repentance. Recognition of the brokenness with which church and synagogue bear witness to the dawning and vision of the messianic age places limitations upon the claims which the church can make about the continuity and *fullness* of its institutions.

C. The Church's Liturgy Communicates the Identity and Mission of the Gospel

43. Shared narrative or story gives a community its identity. The identity of the Christian community is determined by the story (history) of the Scriptures with its climax in Jesus as the Christ. That story in turn shapes the three dimensions of the community's life: its *liturgy* or worship, its *polity* or disciplined life together, and its *doctrine* or normative teaching. All three terms—liturgy, polity, and doctrine—include aspects of the church's life in their definitions. Liturgy is worship. Etymologically, however, liturgy means one's duties as a citizen, that is, engaging in both the rites and responsibilities of citizenship. Participation in the church's liturgy entails ethics and mission as well as sharing in the rites of worship. Polity means more than governance. It means how the whole life together of the community is shaped by and witnesses to its story. Doctrine is, of course, normative teaching and includes the church's creeds, dogmas, and authorized proclamation. Doctrine, however, is to be understood not as a body of theory divorced from

the common life of the church, but as what defines and makes sense of the church's story. The credibility of the church as witness to the gospel in its liturgy, polity, and doctrine is necessarily affected by the way it lives (cf. John 17:20-21). *Martyria,* it must be remembered, means "witness," but it soon and validly came to mean the witness of giving one's life as testimony that the power to inflict death was not the final power, that there was more to do with life than to prolong it. Attention is given to the church's life as mission in Section 5 of this document.

44. The Eucharist is the normative rite of the community of the baptized gathered for worship on the Lord's day. It is the rite by which the church is identified as the eschatological people of God and which shapes the church's mission of witness to the breaking in of the reign of God. In the last meal with the Twelve just before his execution, Jesus identifies the bread and the cup with his imminent death and promises his participation with the Twelve in the messianic meal of the inbreaking reign of God (Matt. 26:20-29; Mark 14:17-25; Luke 22:14-23). Both the eschatological hope of Israel as well as the *meal* dimension of Jesus' ministry are among the significant factors which provide the context for understanding the last meal. The prophet Isaiah sees the consummation of Israel's history in terms of a feast on Mount Zion to which all peoples will come when God has swallowed up death forever and wiped away tears from all faces (Isa. 25:6-8).

45. Because Jesus both made implicit messianic claims and was perceived to be making messianic claims by his contemporaries, the feedings of multitudes (Matt. 14:13-21 and parallels) are perceived and retold as messianic actions (cf. especially John 6:14-15). Jesus also uses the meal as a part of his ministry in his teaching about his messianic mission (Matt. 8:11-12; Luke 13:28-30; Matt. 22:1-10; Luke 14:15-24) and

his gathering of the lost sheep of Israel; for his eating with tax collectors and sinners was characteristic enough to become a primary accusation against him (Luke 15:1-2; cf. Ezek. 34:1-24). In the community that gathers as the consequence of and witness to the resurrection of Jesus, the meal is central (Acts 2:42, 46). "The breaking of bread" functions as a designation for the Eucharist in the Lukan literature. Paul deals explicitly with the Lord's Supper in 1 Corinthians (e.g., 5:6-8; 10:14-22; 11:17-34), and the remaining letters of Paul together with other documents of the New Testament such as the Revelation to John presuppose the Eucharist. What all of this means is that from the beginning the community of Jesus' disciples understood itself to be the eschatological people of God and celebrated the Eucharist as the messianic banquet. The Eucharist is thus the rite through which the baptized continually receive the promise of the Christ that they are the community of the reign of God and are continually sent into the mission of the Christ on behalf of the reign of God.

46. In *Baptism, Eucharist and Ministry,* the document of the Faith and Order Commission of the World Council of Churches, all of the interpretive themes of the Eucharist are related to the eschatological identity of the people of God. The Eucharist is (A) *thanksgiving* "for everything that God will accomplish in bringing the Kingdom to fulfillment." It thus "signifies what the world is to become: an offering and hymn of praise to the Creator, a universal communion in the body of Christ, a kingdom of justice, love and peace in the Holy Spirit." The Eucharist is (B) an *anamnesis,* a remembering to which Christ has attached the promise of his presence and thus "the foretaste of his *parousia* and of the final kingdom." The Eucharist is (C) the *invocation of the Spirit,* that is, the divine presence and power of the new age through which "the Church receives the life of the new creation and the assurance of the Lord's return." The Eucharist is (D) the *communion* of the

faithful, demonstrating and effecting "the oneness of the sharers with Christ and with their fellow sharers in all times and places." In the Eucharist "the community of God's people is fully manifested." Finally, the Eucharist is (E) the *meal of the kingdom,* the foretaste of the *eschaton,* "the church's participation in God's mission to the world" (*Baptism, Eucharist and Ministry,* Part II, Eucharist, pars. 2-26).

47. Two themes are of particular significance for our churches. Lutherans have historically emphasized the "real presence" of Christ's body and blood for the forgiveness of sins as the heart and center of the gospel character of the Eucharist. The intent behind such an emphasis was to trust the word and promise of Christ, assuring the faithful that it is not their believing which gives meaning to the bread and cup but rather the objective body and blood promised by Christ which is offered to them. In short, faith does not effect the presence of Christ; rather, it receives the promise of Christ. We confess and affirm that the "once-for-all-time" offering of Christ, his body and blood, which has overcome the reign of sin and death and has inaugurated the final reign of God, is present, distributed to, and received by all who participate in the Eucharistic meal. Faith trusts the promise that sin is forgiven, that the reign of life has begun.

48. Episcopalians have historically emphasized that the Eucharist, as "the Church's sacrifice of praise and thanksgiving, is the way by which the sacrifice of Christ is made present, and in which he unites us to his one offering of himself" (*Book of Common Prayer,* p. 859). The intent behind such emphasis is to recognize that God initiates and offers expiation for sin in the sacrifice of Christ, the fruits of which are made available to us as an expression of God's gracious initiative and will to save. Christians receive this blessing of God through faith, not calling into question the historical uniqueness and completion,

the "once-for-all-time" character, of Christ's sacrifice on the cross. Lutherans can understand and appropriate this emphasis in terms of the words of Swedish Bishop Gustaf Aulen:

> When the living Lord meets his own in Holy Communion, he actualizes the sacrifice anew in the gifts of bread and wine. As the Lord on the last evening included and incorporated his disciples in his sacrifice of love about to be perfected in death, so now he includes his disciples everywhere and in all times in the eternally valid sacrifice in the new covenant established in his death. This participation involves dying to the old age and walking in the newness of life. In this sense it involves "dying with Christ" and "living in the power of His resurrection" (Phil. 3:10). The sacrifice of Christ is victory. The Lord who is present in the Lord's Supper and there deals with his church is the heavenly Victor.[5]

In contemporary ecumenical dialogue, Lutherans have agreed that in the Lord's Supper Christ is present "as the once-for-all sacrifice for the sins of the world who gives himself to the faithful," and that "the celebration of the eucharist is the church's sacrifice of praise and self-offering or oblation." We therefore confess and affirm that in the Eucharist we share in Christ's "once-for-all-time" offering through faith's praise and thanksgiving, a praise and thanksgiving whose most faithful expression is that we are set free by Christ to offer ourselves as living sacrifices, taken up into his mission in and for the world (Rom. 12:1-2).[6]

49. In the Eucharist the church receives and renews not only its identity but also the shape of its mission. The church is called to be a witness to the breaking in of the *eschaton*. It is not only identified by the body of Christ which it receives in the Eucharistic meal; it is called to be the body of Christ in and for the world. It not only receives the benefits of Christ's

death and resurrection; when it eats and drinks in the Eucharistic meal, it proclaims the Lord's death until he comes (1 Cor. 11:26). The themes of eschatological identity and mission come to special expression in the Gospel of John.

> He who eats my flesh and drinks my blood has eternal life, and I will raise him up at the last day. For my flesh is food indeed, and my blood is drink indeed. He who eats my flesh and drinks my blood abides in me, and I in him. As the living Father *sent* me, and I live because of the Father, so he who eats me will live because of me.
>
> (John 6:54-57, italics added)

The purpose of St. Paul's invoking of the liturgical tradition, the narrative of the Last Supper (1 Cor. 11:23-25), was to recall the Corinthian church to its mission, its embodiment of the gospel, which it was denying when the more affluent did not share food with the less affluent. Because death and all that it symbolizes has been overcome in Jesus Christ, because death no longer has the last word for the community of faith in Jesus Christ, the church is nourished in its identity as witness to the reign of God and is thereby enabled to participate sacrificially in that transformation of the world which is the purpose of God's redemptive act in Jesus (John 3:16-17). On the basis of the gospel which it celebrates in the Eucharist, the church is called and enabled to serve the humanity and creation restored to the reign of God in Jesus Christ. The quality of that service should disclose in the world a more faithful stewardship of creation and a more authentic existence before God and in community with others than is possible on the terms of the powers dominated by death.

50. The Eucharist is the church's ritual narration of the story of Jesus, the eschatological meal in which the gathered people of God participate. The church is thus identified as Christ's

end-time community and receives a Christ-like shape to its mission. Such an understanding not only serves to explain the centrality of the Eucharist in the life of the earliest church. It also provides the theological rationale for the recovery of the Eucharist as the normal Sunday liturgy for parishes today (cf. *Baptism, Eucharist and Ministry,* Part II, Eucharist, Par. 31). A significant implication of the gospel is the weekly and festival celebration of the Eucharist. We therefore urge the parishes of our respective churches to move deliberately and consciously toward renewal of the Eucharistic liturgy. That would mean celebration of the Eucharist at all Sunday and Festival gatherings of the people of the parish. The *Book of Common Prayer,* p. 13, identifies "The Holy Eucharist" as "the principal act of Christian worship on the Lord's Day and other major Feasts." The *Statement on Communion Practices* of The American Lutheran Church and the Lutheran Church in America, Par. II.B.2., quotes the Apology of the Augsburg Confession, Article 24,1: "In our churches Mass is celebrated every Sunday and on other festivals when the Sacrament is offered to those who wish for it after they have been examined and absolved." Then the statement continues: "Congregations are encouraged to move toward this goal because the complete service of Holy Communion embodies the fullness of the Means of Grace, because it provides an excellent *focus for the whole Christian life and mission,* and because it witnesses to our confessional and ecumenical heritage" (italics added). Within a broader context, the recovery of the liturgy of the various members of the church needs to be continually promoted, so that the church can be freed of both clericalism and anti-clericalism, the whole people can be newly empowered for ministry, and the roles of all can be interdependently valued.

D. The Church's Polity Is Life Together for Witness to the Gospel.

51. This topic confronts our churches with the most obvious, although not the only, obstacle to full communion not only

because there are actual differences in governance and ordination between our churches but also because there are differences in understanding the function of bishops and in the significance attached to the historic episcopate. When polity is understood in terms of specific forms, such understanding determines the way our respective churches raise questions about it. To Lutherans it seems that Episcopalian emphasis on the historic episcopate and its authority to ordain could be an unwarranted addition to the gospel. To Episcopalians the Lutheran view that, when there is agreement on the gospel, polity can become an *adiaphoron* seems an unwarranted indifference with regard to something that is at least an implication of the gospel. In this document we will not deal with all the issues related to polity. Another document of this dialogue will be devoted to the group of topics mandated by the 1982 resolutions authorizing Interim Sharing of the Eucharist, namely, "historic episcopate, and ordering of ministry (bishops, priests, and deacons) in the total context of apostolicity." If we understand polity as disciplined life together, then we can here give an account of how the gospel defines and shapes the polity of the church; how, in fact, the polity of the church is an implication of the gospel.

52. Polity is normally defined as a "politically organized community." But if the gospel is that the reign of God has begun and will triumph, then this cannot mean politics as usual. "You know that those who are supposed to rule over the Gentiles lord it over them, and their great men exercise authority over them. *But it shall not be so among you*" (Mark 10:42-43, italics added). Hence, polity in the church must mean the visible life together of the community which believes that Jesus is the Christ, that the messianic age has begun, that the reign of God will finally triumph. Polity includes governance, but it is more than governance. It includes the ordering of ministries, but it is more than the ordering of ministries. It is the way the church

as the body of Christ under historical conditions is freed by the gospel so to live together so that the patterns and powers of its life reflect and witness to the reign of God rather than to the patterns and powers of the "old age." Polity in the church thus testifies to the fact that the gospel gives life to a visible, historical community. Further, polity reflects to the church and the world at large the church's utter dependence on the one gospel. We therefore confess and affirm that the church witnesses to the gospel by the way its members live together, that the way its members live together should reflect both the resurrection victory of Jesus and his way of ministry up to and including the cross. Hence polity is fundamentally the gift of discipleship in its essential corporate dimension. The Messiah serves the people of God, calls that people to be the seed bed of the new reconciled and reconciling humanity, and shapes that people's life and mission by the power and character of his own ministry.

53. Two characteristics of Jesus' teaching about the ministry of the messianic community are represented by the terms "to send" *(apostellein)* and "to serve" *(diakonein).*[7] Because Jesus is sent as the Christ by the Father, he sends the community which confesses him as the Christ with his same mission (Mark 9.37 and parallels; Matt. 10:5-15 and parallels; John 3:17; 4:38; 17:3,8,18,21,23,25; 20:21). In a certain sense the church's "apostolicity" *is* its mission, the subject of Section 5 of this document. Equally important is the way the church engages in its mission. *Diakonia* "is the service performed for the unifying and preservation of the church, the service which establishes and maintains the faith."[8] In contrast to secular rule the church was not to be constituted by coercive power. Nor was it to be constituted by learned power (I Cor. 1:18-25), by magical power (Acts 8:18-24; Acts 16:16-24), or religious power (Heb. 13:10-l6). Rather, Jesus brings in the reign of God as the one who serves (Luke 22:27 and parallels; John 13:1-20).

The reign of God did not come through visible power. It came through one who was a slave for slaves, one who was poor for the poor, one who was a servant for servants.[9] Even those who have been given the charism of leadership exercise their leadership "in the Lord" (1 Thess. 5:12-13), as those whose worship is to present themselves as living sacrifices (Rom. 12:1-8, esp. 7 and 8).

54. Both mission and servanthood are characterized by diversity of concrete expression in the New Testament and other writings which take us well into the 2nd Century C.E.[10] The Twelve, resident in Jerusalem, represent a corporate apostolate which witnessed to the messiahship of Jesus within Judaism and kept the emerging Gentile mission in contact with its Jewish matrix. Side by side was the ministry of the Seven (Acts 6–8), often regarded as the origin of the diaconate but more accurately described as a missionary ministry similar to an apostolate like that of Paul. Many of the Pauline churches were apparently led by a presbyter-bishop, while the corporate leadership of elders, derived from synagogue administration, seems to have functioned in the churches described by Luke and the Pastoral Epistles. The leadership of presbyters persisted even at Rome until well into the second century, long after the monarchical episcopate had established itself in Syria and Asia Minor. These offices did not exhaust the forms ministry took in earliest Christianity, for there is abundant evidence of the importance of "charismatic" leaders in both the Pauline (1 Corinthians 12–14; Romans 12; Ephesians 4) and Johannine traditions (1 John 2:20-27; 4:1; 3 John 9-10; Rev. 1:9-11).

55. The unity and reconciliation effected by the inbreaking reign of God embraces a fruitful, but sometimes turbulent, diversity among us. The church, from the beginning, knew a rich variety of activities in its life together, some of which served particularly to undergird its unity. We list a few of these.

a. *The sharing of goods* with those in need is held up in the New Testament writings as a characteristic of church life. Luke describes the earliest community in Jerusalem as exceptionally generous (Acts 4:32—5:11); Paul, later on, collected an offering from churches of his founding to help that church in a time of need (e.g., 2 Corinthians 8–9); and the letters of John (1 John 3:16-18) and James (1:26-27) insist on such sharing as a fundamental Christian duty.

b. *Intercessory prayer* focused the Christians' concern for one another. Paul, for example, asked for such prayers for himself from the church at Rome (Rom. 15:30).

c. *Admonition and correction* were devoted to preserving community among those in disagreement. To accuse is to expose an enemy and break community. To admonish is to love a friend and preserve community in the midst of conflicts. Thus Paul could rebuke Peter (Gal. 2:11-15) without, it seems, breaking their partnership in the gospel.

d. *Suffering* for the sake of the gospel, for the sake of the community, also served to further the word of proclamation (Acts 5:41; 2 Cor. 6:4-5; 11:23-29; Col. 1:24-29).

e. *Love and humility* were prominent themes of moral exhortation, for, by putting others first, we promote the unity of the church (1 Corinthians 13; Phil. 2:1-11; 1 John 4:20; Mark 10:42-45).

In these and other ways, the church sought to practice the unity which is one of its cardinal characteristics (John 17:20-21) without obliterating the diversity which made its life vital.

56. In addition to mission, servanthood, diversity, and unity as dimensions of the church's life together, there is still another dimension that we believe can also be found in the life of the early church. A contemporary description of it is found in the agreed statement of Lutherans and Catholics in Dialogue V, *Papal Primacy and the Universal Church,* p. 20, which identifies collegiality and subsidiarity as norms for the renewal of

the church's polity in general and the office of universal pastor in particular.

> *Collegial responsibility* for the unity of the church . . . is of utmost importance in protecting those values which excessive centralization of authority would tend to stifle. . . . The collegial principle calls all levels of the church to share in the concern and responsibilities of leadership for the total life of the church.
>
> The *principle of subsidiarity* is no less important. Every section of the church, each mindful of its special heritage, should nurture the gifts it has received from the Spirit by exercising its legitimate freedom. What can properly be decided and done in smaller units of ecclesial life ought not to be referred to church leaders who have wider responsibilities. Decisions should be made and activities carried out with a participation as broad as possible from the people of God. Initiatives should be encouraged in order to promote a wholesome diversity in theology, worship, witness, and service. All should be concerned that, as the community is built up and its unity strengthened, the rights of minorities and minority viewpoints are protected within the unity of faith.

57. It should be evident from the preceding paragraphs that the earliest centuries of the church's history hold before us a rich vision of the church's polity as life together in response to the gospel. Measuring its current life in terms of these examples, the church confesses by the power of the gospel that it exists in a broken and anticipatory form. It confesses its brokenness in its relation to Judaism; its own disunity; its too frequent identification with oppressing establishments; its failures of compassion, peacemaking, justice, inclusivity, stewardship, and pastoral discipline. The power of the gospel is seen not only in the church's freedom to confess its brokenness and sin but also in its freedom for reform. Indeed, the refusal

to undertake evident and necessary reform is a possible indication that a community has hardened itself against the gospel. The ordination of women by our churches is a specific example of a recently undertaken reform. The importance of this action as an example of how our polity is a witness to the gospel of the reign of God calls for lengthier treatment.

58. The Lima statement, *Baptism, Eucharist and Ministry,* recognizes the role of both men and women in Christian ministry.

> Where Christ is present, human barriers are being broken. The Church is called to convey to the world the image of a new humanity. There is in Christ no male or female (Gal. 3:28). Both women and men must discover together their contributions to the service of Christ in the Church. The church must discover the ministry which can be provided by women as well as that which can be provided by men. A deeper understanding of the comprehensiveness of ministry which reflects the interdependence of men and women needs to be more widely manifested in the life of the Church (p. 23, par. 18).

At the same time the Lima statement acknowledges that there is disagreement regarding the ordination of women. Lutheran and Episcopal churches in the United States have been ordaining women since the 1970s. Yet there is disagreement on this issue not only between our churches and those which do not ordain women but also within our churches and within our dialogue. We are encouraged by the fact that the Roman Catholic Church has expressed the willingness to continue the discussion of this topic and that the Orthodox churches have continued dialogue with us.

59. We on our part are mindful of the necessity of continuing to identify the profound doctrinal reasons which led us to ordain

women. Such theological explication needs to be undertaken not only in order to inform our partners in ecumenical conversation but also to help us reappropriate what our churches have done. While social and cultural forces have obviously created a climate of readiness for the ordained ministry of women, our churches have not acted simply as a concession to such social and cultural forces. We have listened to the concerns of our ecumenical partners, but we have above all been persuaded by the freedom for radical newness given to women and men in Christ and by the Holy Spirit's gift of ministry so evidently bestowed on women and men.

60. There are statements in the New Testament, notably 1 Cor. 14:34-36 and 1 Tim. 2:11-15, which reflect the practice of the Greco-Roman culture or perpetuate the synagogue tradition of not admitting women to roles of public leadership or witness. However, other statements of the New Testament, e.g., Gal. 3:27-28, indicate that in the new age inaugurated by the resurrection of Jesus new possibilities are open to women and men in their relationship to each other and in ministries within the eschatological community. The Gospels indicate that Jesus related to women in a new way (Luke 7:36-50; Luke 10:38-42; Mark 14:3-9; Matt. 26:6-13; John 4:4-42; John 20:1, 11-18) and that from Easter onwards, whether as witnesses to the resurrection of Jesus or as participants in the orders of widows, deacons, prophets, teachers, and apostles, women exercised significant ministry in and for the church. In Christ the alienations and oppressions related to gender are overcome. The differences within the documents of the New Testament point to the observation that Gal. 3:28 identifies the *agenda* for the community of the new age: "There is neither Jew nor Greek, there is neither slave nor free, there is neither male nor female; for you are all one in Christ Jesus." The Church is called to wrestle with the implementation of this agenda against the powers of the "old age." The New Testament documents are

themselves evidence that the struggle of the "new age" in Christ against slavery and economic oppression, against ethnic and racial oppression, against sexism and gender oppression has not always, perhaps not often, been successful. But it remains the agenda.

61. Although Jesus appointed men to the Twelve, their ministry to Israel was as an eschatological sign (cf. par. 39, above). The New Testament, however, does not identify the function of the Twelve in terms of presiding at the Eucharist nor does it identify Christ's maleness as a quality which is necessary for those who preside at the Eucharist. Jesus identifies his own ministry as the Christ with the decision to be servant, not master (Mark 10:45 and parallels), and with the determination to offer himself sacrificially. The presence and presidency of Christ in the Eucharist has to do with the grace, forgiveness, and sacrificial servant love which frees his community to enter into his way of being in the world. Such presence and presidency is not about gender, much less the domination and oppression which has often been associated with gender.

62. We are mindful of the fact that long centuries of tradition have excluded women from ordained ministry. While the churches provided women with opportunities not generally available to them in other areas of society, it is also true that the history of the church is replete with evidence of the denigration of women in the church (e.g., the accusation that women are the original and continuing cause of sin[11]) and of the domination and oppression of women by men. As churches that have participated in the conservative reformation of the 16th century, we bear witness to the concern that what we have inherited ought not be arbitrarily rejected. But we are also convinced that the historical antiquity of a practice is no guarantee of its validity and that no practice is beyond challenge and reform. We believe that the practice of ordaining only men

must be challenged in the name of the gospel, that it is part of the brokenness of the church in history to have excluded women from ordained ministry. We believe that whenever women have been included in the ordained ministries of the church it represents a significant development in the church's struggle against the powers of the "old age." It is an act of fidelity to the tradition of the *imago Dei* as comprehending both "male and female" (Gen. 1:26-28).

63. Our attempt to discern the implications for polity of the gospel of the reign of God is part of our effort to manifest our visible unity through full communion. We do not yet know whether or how this might take place between churches with and without the historic episcopate. In addition to the example of the early church and the major reform action described above we have before us helpful ecumenical suggestions such as the final paragraphs of *Baptism, Eucharist and Ministry* (pars. 51-55), and the significant proposal of the Roman Catholic/Lutheran Joint Commission, *Facing Unity.* Our current agreement commits us to the quest for full communion. It is clear that the quest will ask of *all* members of our churches just that "lowliness and meekness," that patience and forbearing of one another in love, for which the author of Ephesians begs.

E. The Church's Doctrine Serves Its Proclamation of the Gospel

64. *Doctrine* means all teaching that is authentically Christian. Doctrinal formulations can function either descriptively ("This is what Christians, in fact, teach") or prescriptively ("This is what Christians ought to teach"). Throughout the centuries of Christian history both functions have been fraught with problems. Prescriptive doctrine has been experienced as oppressive, obscurantist, stagnating, inhibiting. It has been the occasion for purges, trials, executions, wars. In our churches the very

concept of prescriptive doctrine evokes different emotional responses. Lutherans have developed an ethos in which there is considerable doctrinal and theological homogeneity, in which there is significant affirmation of prescriptive doctrine. Episcopalians have developed an ethos in which there is considerable doctrinal and theological variety, in which there is less sense of a prescriptive doctrinal tradition, but a greater importance attached to the role of descriptive doctrine. In the face of both historical difficulties and differences in ethos we must proceed carefully so that what we can and must affirm is both clear and persuasive.

65. We can and must affirm the concept of normative doctrine because what is at stake is the authenticity of the church's proclamation, that is, the authenticity of the church's gospel. What *is* being proclaimed as gospel in the church dare not automatically be identified with what *ought* to be proclaimed as gospel. Hence the concept of normative doctrine requires the church to struggle with the question of the authenticity of its gospel and the quality or faithfulness of its proclamation. The church is called to be the witness in word and deed to God's own vision for the world, God's promise to the world, God's ultimate gift to the world. The purpose of normative doctrine is not to be the guardian of institutional ideology. The purpose is rather to evaluate the quality and consequence of the church's proclamation. Are the church's words good news for the poor, liberation to captives, light for those who sit in darkness, life for those whose existence is overshadowed by death? When speaking about the normative doctrine of the gospel, the key words are *normative* and *gospel*. There *is* a gospel, hence there is *normative* doctrine; but it is *gospel*, hence anything said or done in the name of the gospel which is death dealing, oppressive, defensive, victimizing, or denigrating is a denial and contradiction of the gospel. Whatever in the church's proclamation does not liberate from the bondage

of sin and death, enkindle the vision of the reign of God, promise the final gift of life everlasting, offer ultimate hope and comfort, or give courage for faithful witness, is not the gospel.

66. The church's call is to witness to God's future for the world, to be the bearer of God's promises for the world. The church is therefore the community of living proclamation. The revision of the church's lectionary, especially the expansion into a three-year cycle for Sundays and Festivals and the addition of a reading from the Old Testament to the lessons for the Eucharist, promises more extensive encounter with the Scriptures than has ever been available in the church's liturgy. However, even this more comprehensive lectionary cannot be a substitute for the living proclamation of the word of God. The Scriptures come to us from the past with a narrative of God's interaction with Israel and God's final redemption in Jesus, the Christ, which we confess to be the Word of God. But the word of God is not and cannot be only a narrative from the past. It is a narrative into which we can and must enter so that it becomes God's present address of judgment and promise here and now. The present word of God is always rooted in and normed by the biblical word; but just as there is no substitute for the normative word of Holy Scripture, so there is no substitute for its contemporary proclamation. The church is called, indeed commanded, to speak God's judgment and promise today (Luke 10:16; 2 Cor. 5:20; Acts 4:20). It cannot simply read the lessons and hope that the congregation will consider itself addressed. The church must make the address explicit. It must also aid the hearers to discriminate, to understand the words of Scripture through which they are being addressed. It is the task of the sermon to show how these words are to be understood and to be applied in the light of Christ and in the context of our situation. It is in living proclamation that Christians are to hear both a discriminating and an empowering word. The

ritual rhetoric of the Christian community is the language by which the community's story is retold so that God's everlasting promises are proclaimed, God's present judgments are announced, and God's saving deeds are remembered and made present. Faith must have Someone to believe. What faith believes is the promise contained in the living Word of God, rooted in the scriptural witness to Jesus as the Christ, preached here and now in the midst of the congregation.

67. The Holy Scriptures are the norm for the church's proclamation of the gospel. That the gospel was at stake is evident from both the liturgical and the polemical contexts for the formation of the biblical canon. With the death of the apostolic generation and the gathering of oral traditions about Jesus into Gospel codices, a body of documents became available for reading in Christian communities gathered for worship. The documents which authenticated themselves in worship were authorized for public use in Eucharistic assemblies. The process of reception by the church, which lasted a number of centuries, also at times involved the heat of controversy. The Marcionite practice of circulating lists of approved documents, excluding not only the Scriptures of Israel (Old Testament) but also many of the documents from the apostolic era (New Testament) was one of the major factors that caused bishops and theologians late in the 2nd century C.E. to begin identifying canonical lists. The church early acknowledged its matrix in Israel and its confession that Jesus is Messiah by including the Scriptures of Israel in its canon of authoritative Scripture. This was a decision about the gospel with far-reaching implications for Israel as well as for those who confess that Jesus is Messiah (see above, par. 42). To the Scriptures of Israel the church added documents with a variety of perspectives on the gospel. But what is even more important, it *excluded* documents. In order to understand fully and authentically what gospel the church means to confess on the basis of its canonical writings,

it is equally important to know what "gospel" or what versions of the gospel are being rejected and excluded. To be sure, not every document that was excluded is antithetical to the gospel of the canonical documents. But what is most important is that the canon of the Scriptures has to do with the gospel. Only the Scriptures of the church give us normative access to the authentic gospel. Only the gospel gives the canonical Scriptures its proper and appropriate authority.

68. Like the canon of the Scriptures, dogma came into being at those points in the church's life where alternatives threatened the gospel itself. The creedal affirmation of the world as creation and God as creator was directed against the Gnostic denial of the goodness of the world. At stake is the proclamation of the reign of God and its affirmation of the world's future, its proclamation that life, not death, will have the final word in the consummation of history. Arising out of the Arian and post-Nicean controversies, the christological and trinitarian dogmas identify the God of the gospel with the person and history of Jesus (see above, Section 2). In the Pelagian controversy the church recognized the universal guilt, the bondage of self-justification or self-hatred, which comes with our origin. At stake was the comfort and liberation that is conferred by the grace of the gospel. Born in the fires of controversy, dogma identifies the mandatory content of the church's teaching and proclamation, that is, it identifies what *must* be said if the gospel is to continue to be proclaimed.

69. In the 16th century leading reformers both on the European continent and in the British Isles were persuaded that the proc-lamation of the gospel was in danger of losing its quality as unconditional promise and that therefore the church's proclamation could no longer evoke the faith which alone receives the gospel as comfort and liberation. Among these reformers

the doctrine of "justification by faith" functioned as a hermeneutical test for church proclamation. The promise of the gospel was to be so unconditionally proclaimed ("We are accounted righteous before God, only for the merit of our Lord and Saviour Jesus Christ by Faith, and not for our own works or deservings." Article 11, Articles of Religion, *Book of Common Prayer,* p. 870) that faith in the promise, not works of self-justification, would be the appropriate response. Our churches still acknowledge the validity of the insights of our Reformation ancestors, but we do so in different ways. The proclamation and teaching of Lutheran clergy and parishes must be measured by the standard of the documents contained in the *Book of Concord* of 1580, especially the catholic creeds, the Augsburg Confession of 1530, and the Small Catechism of Martin Luther. In Episcopal parishes the use of the *Book of Common Prayer* is mandated by canon law. The rites and liturgical materials prescribed by the *Book of Common Prayer* function as a standard by which worship, including the administration of the sacraments, as well as doctrine itself, must be measured. Each church can and should ask significant questions of the other and indeed of itself. How, if at all, does the *Book of Concord* shape the worship, including administration of the sacraments, in Lutheran parishes? How, if at all, does the *Book of Common Prayer* shape proclamation and teaching in Episcopal parishes? What is significant in the very asking of these questions is the fact that both churches want to be held accountable for the authenticity of the gospel in the life of the church.

70. This area of the church's life and mission in faithfulness to the gospel provides ample opportunity for the exercise of humility. The relationship between the church and the reign of God is not one of identity. By the church's own confession of faith God is Lord of history as well as of the church (Rev. 11:15). The redeeming reign of God can manifest itself in the

world, and as a witness to that reign the church is called to discern and acknowledge the fact. This has important implications for the style of evangelization employed by the church. The living Word of God, Jesus Christ, is not imported by Christians or the church into persons or cultures from which God's witness is absent; but, rather, what is surely there inchoately, unclearly, and/or in distorted form is to be brought by true evangelism into completeness, clarity, and/or authenticity in those persons or cultures to whom the church proclaims the gospel (e.g., Acts 14:8-18). The recognition that the reign of God is larger than the church dare not immobilize the church or inhibit its witness. As the explicit bearer of the gospel and its principal implication in history, the church is called in every time and place faithfully to fulfill its life and mission. The world, with all the questions that it poses for church and gospel, is the locus as well as the object of the church's witness to the reign of God.

IV. The *World* and the Gospel

A. The Contemporary World

71. The term *world* has been troublesome because it has a variety of meanings in the New Testament, most notably in the Gospel of John. There it means at times all that is hostile to the Christ (e.g., John 15:18-19) and therefore the antithesis to Christ's way of being (e.g., John 18:36-37); or, at other times, it means the object of God's love (e.g., John 3:16-17) and Christian witness (John 17:21-23). Sometimes *world* is simply a neutral designation for the universe or whatever exists (e.g., John 1:10; 9:32). We have at times used the term *world* as a synonym for the universe; but most often we have used it to refer to the "cultural context" within which the church exists and which it is called to address. One major dimension of the world as cultural context is the post-Enlightenment phenomenon known as "secularity." While secularity is complex and has taken on many forms, including hostility to religion and persecution of religious communities, the form or facet of secularity which must be of particular concern to Western Christians is the way it has called into question the public meaningfulness of religious language. This is especially important for churches in the United States of America.

72. Although religious institutions have persisted in the United States and, in contrast to other Western countries, even experienced remarkable growth since the end of World War II, religion is regarded by many as an essentially private or "personal" experience. The central terms and themes of religion,

God, revelation, and *salvation,* are no longer public terms giving thematic expression to common ways of experiencing the world. As language for individual or subgroup experiences, the terms are relativized ("what God means to me"). Although its institutions are thriving, a relativized religion is a contradiction in terms since the term *God* means, at the very least, whoever or whatever can make a universal and unconditional claim upon us. Secularity as the privatization of religion thus challenges the church's very ability to address the world meaningfully with a public word.

73. The global consciousness which modern travel and communication have made possible and the interdependence which modern business and industry necessitate have made Western Christians more aware of world religions and greatly complicated our way of relating to world religions. The statistics from the *World Christian Encyclopedia,* edited by David B. Barrett (Oxford University Press, 1982) are striking: In the past 50 years Christianity has increased numerically by more than 50%, to more than one and a quarter billion Christians. But its *proportion* of the world's population has *decreased* from about 33% to less than 26%. The great non-Christian world religions meanwhile have doubled in size (Islam has actually tripled) and have maintained their proportion of the world's population, about 42%.

74. At the beginning of this century Christians had an uncomplicated strategy for relating to non-Christians: service and evangelism. Western Christians also had ready access to most countries of the world. However, with the Russian revolution at the end of World War I, and the end of the colonial empires together with the establishment of a marxist-socialist government in the People's Republic of China at the end of World War II, Western missionary activity has been banned or severely restricted in many parts of Asia and Africa. Western

Christians have increasingly come to ask whether and how the gospel can be addressed to a post-colonial world, and in the midst of resurgent, vital world religions.

75. Meanwhile Western secular culture has experienced a phenomenon often called "the return of enchantment," a reaction to the sterile rationalism of scientific and technological modernity. Fantasy, myth, and magic have regained popularity. Astrology, occultism, cults, new religions, and variations of old religions have won new adherents and have gained new visibility in publishing, entertainment, the media, and public consciousness. The increasing popularity of religious and quasi-religious phenomena, the increasing interest in the transcendental and the supernatural, both confirm some Christian claims and insights about the religious character of human beings and challenge contemporary Christianity's capacity to respond to the religious dimension. In this area Christian discernment is required. A "baptized imagination" (C.S. Lewis) enriches theological reflection, whereas uncritical use of imagination in theology and religion can lead to superstition or sentimentality.

76. Christian churches, including our own, have experienced new movements and the renewal of earlier movements. Liturgical renewal, interest in "spiritual direction," small group gatherings for home Bible study, liberation movements, and attention to peace and justice issues have proliferated in the churches. Three movements have been especially prominent among Christians in the United States. Renewed Evangelicalism has surfaced in televised revivals, large metropolitan "crusades," and home visitation evangelism programs. Renewed Fundamentalism has advanced its own political agenda and pressed for legislation in such areas as school prayer, censorship, sexual behavior, and the teaching of "scientific creationism." The Charismatic movement has stressed the miraculous response to prayer, a direct and ecstatic experience of

the Holy Spirit, direct divine guidance for life decisions, and spiritual renewal of the church.

77. The paradoxical consequence of these latter three movements has been both negative and positive. Many aspects of modern learning have been rejected, often to the point of establishing militantly separatistic educational institutions, and all too often it has seemed that these movements do little more than provide simplistic justifications for a rather shallow nationalism as well as a rather narrow orientation towards this-worldly success in business and politics. On the other hand, it cannot be denied that these movements have spread at least one version of the Christian message, have brought many outsiders to some acquaintance with Jesus, have stimulated interest in the words of Holy Scripture, and have given to many persons a newfound life in the Spirit of Christ.

78. It is the conviction of the churches represented by this document that the church has both the call and the capacity to address the world. The gospel is the proclamation of God's inbreaking future, an alternative to other anticipations of the future, whether secular or religious. The gospel is a vision of God's goal for history which is grounded in Jesus, the Christ. Attention to the grounding of the gospel in the biblical witness to Jesus (Section 1), to the gospel's God characterized by the person and history of Jesus (Section 2), and to the church as the eschatological community called to witness to the reign of God (Section 3), articulates an understanding of the gospel which has three consequences. First, it can be meaningful and intelligible in the context of a secular worldview. Second, it calls human beings to an authentic spirituality. Third, it aids Christians in discriminating among strategies for relating to the universe. It is the task of the following paragraphs to describe a strategy for addressing the world which we believe to be both faithful and meaningful.

B. The Gospel Vision: The World as Creation

79. The term *creation* as used in Christian theology is neither a philosophical nor a scientific term. Rather, it is a theological statement, that is, a statement about the universe in relation to God, the creator. It is a theological assertion grounded in the gospel, a way of saying that God the creator brings order out of chaos, light out of darkness, life out of death. When the gospel asserts that the universe is creation, it identifies the Christian doctrine of creation as a major implication of the gospel. Israel's experience and remembrance of the Exodus deliverance are the basis for the way it regards the universe, confesses the universe as belonging to God, and rejoices in the goodness of the universe (e.g., Deut. 26:1-11). The prophet of the exile proclaims that the God who comforts and forgives Israel is the creator of the universe (Isa. 40:1-31; 45:1-19). The people of God who have experienced renewal and redemption in Jesus, the Christ, confess him as the *Logos* through whom "all things were made" (John 1:3), as the "image of the invisible God" through whom and for whom "all things were created" and in whom "all things hold together" (Col. 1:15-18). The Christian good news is neither a negation of the world nor an attempt to escape the world. It is an affirmation of the world.

80. The God proclaimed as Savior in Jesus, the Christ, is a God of sovereign freedom. But God's freedom is not freedom *from* the universe, i.e., a God unaffected by time and space. Rather, God's freedom is freedom to be *for* the universe. Hence the universe is not an unintended emanation from God's being. Rather, it is *creation,* that is, that which is intended by God's love, by God's being as love. By confessing God as creator the church is affirming about God's relationship to space what it already believes about God's relationship to time on the basis of its encounter with Jesus: God loves life and wills into existence that which is not God. As contingent being the world

as creation exists *vis-à-vis* God. It is both dependent upon and other than God.

81. By confessing the universe as creation Christians affirm its goodness, its fecundity, its variety, its processes of development and inner creativity, its pleasures, and the natural happiness it affords. Christians confess that human beings have the potential to share in God's creative freedom. Their ability to transcend the instinctual necessities of organic and animal life gives them the capacity to understand, shape, and transform the world. That this potential and capacity has often gone disastrously awry is self-evident. The gospel grounding of the Christian doctrine of creation calls human beings to the freedom of stewardship in relation to the universe, the freedom to bring creation into existence out of our universe. The freedom to "name" other creatures (Gen. 2:19) is the gift of understanding, using, and serving the universe with a steward's care. The universe awaits and benefits from the eschatological salvation of humanity (Rom. 8:18-25).

C. The Gospel and Evil

82. The Christian doctrine of creation means that the gospel must be proclaimed in the face of evil. A contingent universe includes death as well as life, disease and pain as well as pleasure and happiness, destructive as well as creative forces. In addition to natural or biological distortion, suffering, and death, there is the perversion of human freedom and stewardship into waste, corruption, oppression, torture, and murder. The reality of evil involves those who confess God as creator and the world as creation in a seeming dilemma: goodness lacks either power or reality; that is, goodness either cannot or will not triumph.

83. The Christian gospel makes three assertions in the face of

evil. First, the freedom of God's creative love means that God accepts the consequences of calling into existence that which is not God. That is always the risk of love. The final freedom of love is the freedom to be hurt by, to suffer through the object of one's love. The freedom to create the universe and to make creation out of the universe is finally the freedom to be vulnerable.

84. Second, God does in fact suffer. That is a theme which is found in the prophetic Scriptures of Israel. That is also the heart of the apostolic Scriptures and the church's dogma: Jesus is the ultimate, the final way God suffers. Here is an alternative to understanding God either as absolute power or absolute indifference. The alternative is that God chooses to be involved as victim. Indeed, salvation or forgiveness occurs in no other way. The God who suffers and dies is available as companion, comfort, and Savior to all who experience the pain of suffering and the dread of death. The people of God believe the good news of God's redemptive suffering as an alternative to despair in the face of evil (1 Peter 2:18-25).

85. Third, in the resurrection of Jesus from death the church recognizes God's affirmation of the cross as the way God's love triumphs over evil. Jesus is the firstborn of a redeemed humanity. He has overcome evil by being its victim. The people of God witness to that by forgiving enemies, suffering with hope, identifying with victims, seeking to liberate oppressors and oppressed alike, supporting nonviolent resistance to evil, working to control and contain the use of violence (see the "just war" doctrine common to most Christian churches which requires that governmental use of violence be accountable and limited, that it be directed only against other combatants, that it be a last resort, that it be understood as the lesser of evils). The promise of the gospel leaves us neither helpless nor hopeless in the face of evil. That is why Christian martyrdom is the ultimate witness *(martyria)* to the gospel.

D. The Gospel and Human Sin

86. Everything is known more profoundly, known for what it really is, in the light of the gospel. Because of the gospel the church recognizes both the power and the reality of sin. Because sin is fundamentally a theological reality, because it is against God and the reign of God, therefore it is not adequately recognized and confessed apart from the gospel. Its recognition and confession belong to the implications of the gospel.

87. Humanity is alienated from the reign of God, from God's call and vision for us as creation. Humanity has fallen from the freedom for love to the bondage of self-absorption or self-hatred. Humanity has fallen prey to the reign of death. The powers that serve death drive us to self-protection at whatever cost to others or to self-hatred at the cost of distortion of the self. We serve the powers of death also and not least in our drive quest for "prosperity" (cf. The Great Litany, *Book of Common Prayer,* p. 149, *Lutheran Book of Worship,* p. 170). Humanity is captive to false gods, heteronomous powers, religious or secular; or it is captive to equally false autonomy, seeking to be a law unto itself. The church recognizes that in the last analysis sin is not so much misbehavior as it is misbelief, faith, and trust directed toward that which is other than God's redeeming reign, resulting in both groundless arrogance or groundless despair. Such misbelief or misdirected orientation means that the whole of our existence, not just individual acts, is guilty existence, existence under condemnation.

88. The good news of the gospel is that God has not abandoned the world. Rather, the Father gave up the Son, and the Son gave himself up to death, and thus God made a final irrevocable commitment to the world. Even God's judgment is a sign that God cares about and cares for the world. Every uncovering of human sin and evil is a prophetic "word of God." Unexpected

as well as expected voices of God's judgment proclaim the ways in which humans pervert and deny the goodness of God's world, oppress others, cling to unwarranted privilege and power at the expense of justice. Recognition of the justice of God's judgment (Ps. 119:75, "I know, O Lord, that thy judgments are right, and that in faithfulness thou hast afflicted me") is a fundamental implication of the gospel.

89. To be grasped by the gospel of the redeeming reign of God is to be free to make God's verdict our own. That is the meaning of repentance: to see matters with a renewed mind; to see matters from the perspective of the gospel rather than to see them from the false perspective of self-preservation or self-hatred (Mark 8:35 and parallels). The meaning of confession is to give up the moralities, legitimations, and self-justifications through which we seek to protect ourselves before God, others, and our own consciences, and equally to give up our unrelenting self-accusation and perfectionism. Confession means to say the same thing *(homologein)* to God that God knows and says to us: that we are sinners. We dare to give up, to confess, because the new repentant mind knows what the old unrepentant mind does not: that God's judgment is penultimate, not ultimate, that God's last word is the forgiving and ennobling *yes.*

90. The good news that God reigns is the costly way of the cross. It is costly for God, who does not give up on the world but gives up for the world. Jesus is the way, the truth, and the life because he gave "his life as a ransom for many" (Mark 10:45 and parallels). Forgiveness is always costly for the forgiver for its means bearing the pain of that which is forgiven. It is costly for the sinner as well, for it means conversion from the old age to the new, from serving the powers of death to serving the power of life, from self-hatred to self-affirmation, from self-preservation to self-offering. That is the path opened

by Baptism, the sacrament of justification. The sinner is plunged into the affirming death and resurrection of Jesus and thus is liberated to undergo the sinner's own death and resurrection. That is also the path celebrated in our Eucharist. We are united with the "once-for-all-time" sacrifice of Jesus so that we become part of God's sacrificial mission for the world.

E. The Gospel as Alternative Vision for the Future of the World

91. Jesus, the Christ, is the grounding of God's future for the world, the future of God's redemptive reign. The author of Ephesians (1:16-23) describes it as follows:

> I do not cease to give thanks for you, remembering you in my prayers, that the God of our Lord Jesus Christ, the Father of glory, may give you a spirit of wisdom and revelation in the knowledge of him, having the eyes of your hearts enlightened, that you may know what is the hope to which he has called you, what are the riches of his glorious inheritance in the saints, and what is the immeasurable greatness of his power in us who believe, according to the working of his great might which he accomplished in Christ when he raised him from the dead and made him sit at his right hand in the heavenly places, far above all rule and authority and power and dominion, and above every name that is named, not only in this age but also in that which is to come; and he has put all things under his feet and has made him the head over all things for the church, which is his body, the fulness of him who fills all in all.

That is the "mystery" from which and for which the people of God live. That is the "secret" of the future of the world: the Christ of suffering and vulnerable love is above "all rule and authority and power and dominion."

92. To proclaim in word, in rite, and in deed the good news

of that future already present in the world is the meaning and function of apostolic ministry. We hear it again in the words of St. Paul.

Therefore, if any one is in Christ, he is a new creation; the old has passed away, behold, the new has come. All this is from God, who through Christ reconciled us to himself and gave us the ministry of reconciliation; that is, in Christ God was reconciling the world to himself, not counting their trespasses against them, and entrusting to us the message of reconciliation. So we are ambassadors for Christ, God making his appeal through us. We beseech you on behalf of Christ, be reconciled to God. For our sake he made him to be sin who knew no sin, so that in him we might become the righteousness of God. Working together with him, then, we entreat you not to accept the grace of God in vain. . . . We put no obstacle in any one's way, so that no fault may be found with our ministry, but as servants of God we commend ourselves in every way: through great endurance, in afflictions, hardships, calamities, beatings, imprisonments, tumults, labors, watching, hunger; by purity, knowledge, forbearance, kindness, the Holy Spirit, genuine love, truthful speech, and the power of God; with the weapons of righteousness for the right hand and for the left; in honor and dishonor, in ill repute and good repute. We are treated as impostors, and yet are true; as unknown, and yet well known, as dying, and behold we live, as punished and yet not killed; as sorrowful, and yet always rejoicing; as poor, yet making many rich; as having nothing, and yet possessing everything.

(2 Cor. 5:17— 6:10).

What is promised to the world is not a cataclysmic future, not a self-indulgent future, not an otherworldly future of individualistic salvation, but the final future of God's reconciling reign. What is promised to the world is not the triumph of the

American revolution, nor the triumph of the Russian revolution, but the final triumph of the Lamb of God whose servant life and death created a reconciled priesthood from "every tribe and tongue and people and nation" (Rev. 5:9-10), a priesthood whose joy and mission and fulfillment witness to God's reign.

V. The *Mission* of the Gospel

A. The Lord's Prayer as the Prayer of Mission

93. Mission is the implication of the gospel *par excellence*. To believe and confess that Jesus is the Christ is to be caught up in his mission, the mission of the reign of God (Matt. 7:21-27; Luke 6:46-49). The people of God struggle with the concrete action which the mission of the reign of God entails when they engage in intercessory prayer in the name of Jesus. To pray in the name of Jesus means nothing else than to be identified with and shaped by his mission and ministry and its promises. That is the significance of the prayer formula known as the Lord's Prayer which Jesus gave his disciples (Luke 11:1-4; Matt. 6:9-13). When the disciples asked Jesus to teach them to pray (Luke 11:1), they were asking for that kind of prayer formula which a rabbi frequently gave his disciples and which then became an identifying mark of their group. Jesus gave his disciples such an identifying prayer. It is at the same time "the clearest and the richest summary of Jesus' proclamation which we possess." [12] Since the content of Jesus' proclamation and ministry is the breaking in of the reign of God, those who use the Lord's Prayer are being shaped for and taken up into his ministry.

94. He teaches his disciples, his community, to call upon his "Abba," his Father. That was the way he addressed the one who had sent him, the one with whose mission in history he is utterly identified (Matt. 11:25-27; Luke 10:21-22; John 5:17, 36; John 6:57; John 13:3; John 20:21). The use of this name

by Jesus is the antithesis of patriarchalism and oppression. Matthew contains a decisive saying about this:

> But you are not to be called rabbi, for you have one teacher, and you are all brethren. And call no man your father on earth, for you have one Father, who is in heaven. Neither be called masters; for you have one master, the Christ. He who is greatest among you shall be your servant; whoever exalts himself will be humbled, and whoever humbles himself will be exalted.
>
> (Matt. 23:8-12)

To be given the "Abba" name is to be called into the *mission* of Jesus and his "Abba," the mission of the reign of God in which and through which alienations and oppressions are overcome.

95. The petitions asking that the name of God be made holy and the kingdom of God come were part of the daily prayer of the synagogue. They were petitions of messianic hope. Jesus now sets them into the context of the fulfillment taking place in his own messianic mission. They are prayed as a cry from the depths by those who know that God's name is profaned and dishonored wherever there is abuse and oppression of people, wherever there are acts of terror and reprisal, wherever there is injustice and hopelessness, wherever there is inequity between the needs of the poor and the means of the rich. To pray these petitions is to recognize the powers of greed and cruelty and vengeance arrayed against God's name and reign. But to pray these petitions also means that we take God's promise seriously, the promise that we live in the time when the turning point has already begun.

96. The proleptic presence of the reign of God is given special expression in the petitions regarding bread and forgiveness. The messianic age will be the triumph of life over death. Jesus

often refers to that age in terms of a banquet in his parables and elsewhere (e.g., Matt. 8:11-12), following the imagery of Isa. 25:6-8. The messianic age finds a special focus in the giving and receiving of the food which nourishes and sustains life. That such sharing of food by the people of God is grounded in the Lord's Supper is self-evident (1 Cor. 11:17-34), for in the Lord's Supper we are anticipating the messianic banquet here and now. Similarly we forgive enemies as an act of trusting not only that God's forgiveness *will be* the final verdict for us but also as a way of trusting that God's forgiveness *is* already ours here and now. As a conclusion Jesus teaches his community to pray that it will be delivered from and in the midst of all assaults which the community will endure because it participates in the mission of Jesus, because it is engaged in witness to the reign of God.

97. All prayer in the name of Jesus grows out of this prayer. No matter with which hopes and fears, needs and desires we begin, if we are praying in the name of Jesus, if our prayers are shaped by the Lord's Prayer, in the end we will be taken up into the ministry and mission of the reign of God. Our life and work, our past and present, our condition and destiny, all are encompassed by the reign of God. In prayer we offer ourselves and seek to discover how and in what concrete form we will be taken up into the mission of the reign of God, trusting the promise of Jesus:

> Ask, and it will be given you;
> seek, and you will find;
> knock, and it will be opened to you.
>
> (Matt. 7:7)

The prayer of the people of God is set into the context of word and sacrament because in worship we receive our identity and mission, the gift of Christ and the vocation of witness. Some concrete dimensions of that mission and witness are here organized around three themes, all of which are equally important and mutually interdependent: ecumenism, evangelism, and ethics.

B. Mission and Ecumenism

98. Repeatedly Christians have confessed that the unity of the church is given, not achieved. The church can only be one because it is constituted by the gospel in word and sacrament, and there is but one gospel. What Christians are seeking when they engage in the tasks and efforts associated with ecumenism is to discover how the unity they have already been given by the gospel can be manifested faithfully in terms of the church's mission. In the often cited prayer of Jesus from the Gospel of John, the unity of the disciple community is to be visible so that the world can know and believe the messianic mission of the Father and the Son and thus participate in the future of the Spirit here and now (John 17:20-26). The goal of the Christ is the gathering of Gentiles to Israel "in one body" (Eph. 2:11-22). To manifest visible unity is the fundamental vocation of the people of God.

> I therefore, a prisoner for the Lord, beg you to lead a life worthy of the calling to which you have been called, with all lowliness and meekness, with patience, forbearing one another in love, eager to maintain the unity of the Spirit in the bond of peace.
>
> (Eph. 4:1-3)

99. Sociological studies of the church have sometimes indicated that attention to ecumenism, especially in the form of visible manifestations of unity, has often resulted in attenuation of mission. Many faithful Christians have concluded that one must choose between ecumenism and evangelism, and they have not hesitated to assign higher priority to the latter. If our

churches must acknowledge the validity of the sociological observations, then one of the concrete and necessary tasks before us is the renewal of our understandings of both unity and mission so that their essential and necessary interdependence is evident in the life of our churches. Whatever Christians can do to manifest that they are indeed "one body" is witness to the presence of the reign of God. Concretely for the Lutheran and Episcopal churches this would mean attention to the following, by no means exhaustive, list of actions.

100. We need to engage in as much common education and shared leadership as possible. Some examples:

a. Might it be possible to share the ministries of staff persons, particularly in the area of parish education, between dioceses of the Episcopal Church and synods of the Evangelical Lutheran Church of America (ELCA)?

b. The formation of the ELCA in 1988 provided for the establishment of nine regional centers for parish life and mission. Is it possible to consider staffing these centers jointly with the Episcopal Church and thus encouraging the use of resources available through such centers to both churches?

c. Might there be provision for a periodic convocation of all bishops from both churches for shared education and mutual consultation?

d. Could we encourage a convocation of seminary deans to arrange for regular exchanges of seminary students and faculty? Perhaps as a beginning visits could be exchanged for periods as brief as a week. Eventually it might be possible for students and faculty from seminaries of one church to spend whole terms at seminaries of the other church.

e. At the present time there are instances of Lutheran faculty persons teaching at Episcopal seminaries and vice versa. Could this practice be expanded beyond the present instances?

f. Could there be periodic conferences of Lutheran and Episcopal theologians?

g. Could there be joint programs of continuing education for clergy of both churches?

h. Might there be encouragement for the clergy of parishes to organize regular, even weekly, gatherings for purposes of mutual prayer, study, and consultation?

i. Could we encourage more Lutheran and Episcopal *parish* covenants as well as more covenants between dioceses and synods so that promising beginnings in this area are rapidly multiplied?

101. We need to cooperate in maintaining and supporting chaplaincies for hospitals, prisons, the military, higher education, and wherever else chaplaincy services are needed or desired. We also need to encourage the cooperation of parishes in particular contexts, e.g., urban situations, for purposes of shared mission and ministry. We also need to cultivate cooperation in establishing new parishes, encouraging shared life and perhaps the use of shared facilities for existing parishes in areas of population decline, and the referring of communicants to one another's parishes in situations where only one of our churches has a parish.

102. Because we already share liturgical traditions that are similar, we need to encourage familiarity with one another's liturgical materials and hymnody. We need to move toward official consultation and common work whenever the revision of our present rites is contemplated. Since both churches have used the texts prepared by the International Consultation on English Texts [ICET] in their revised rites, we should encourage parishes to use and learn the ICET text for the Lord's Prayer. Learning it together would give English speaking Christians a common text for the Lord's Prayer for the first time since the Reformation of the 16th century.

103. We need to continue work towards a shared ecumenical strategy. Some steps might involve occasional joint meetings of the official commissions responsible for ecumenical relationships, inviting representatives from each other's churches to sit on ecumenical and other appropriate commissions, inviting representatives from each other's churches to attend national conventions, coordinating as much as possible the structures for ecumenical work in our respective dioceses and synods.

104. It would be desirable for both churches to become familiar with each other's histories. Since both churches have a number of commemorations in their respective calendars, it would be helpful to make these calendars available in some way to all clergy and parishes. Eventually we should move toward a common list of commemorations. We can also engage in regular and disciplined prayer for each other, the more specific the better. Helpful would be the practice of having each parish pray for one parish and its clergy from the other church. We ought to pray by name for bishops from each other's churches, for specific schools and mission communities, for churches from each other's communions in other countries. Most helpful would be offerings of money and time for each other's ministries, for by such concrete steps we would develop knowledge of and interest in one another, support for one another, dependence upon one another.

105. It should be noted that all of these steps can be taken prior to the actual realization of full communion. None of these steps imply that we have resolved all questions related to full communion. However, these steps would insure that the eventual realization of full communion would reflect an actual sharing of life and mission. We are using the term "full communion" as a synonym for "altar and pulpit fellowship" and

communio in sacris (c.f., the mandating resolution for LED III cited in par. 1 above).

C. Mission and Evangelization

106. The good news of the prophet of the exile was, "Your God reigns" (Isa. 52:7-10). The good news of Jesus was, "The kingdom of God is at hand" (Mark 1:15). The good news of the church can be stated as "Jesus, the crucified one, is the Christ, and the promise of the final triumph of the reign of God cannot be defeated because Jesus has been raised from the dead." The church witnesses to the good news through its words (doctrine, confession, proclamation), worship (liturgy, baptism, eucharist) and deeds (polity, life together, ethic). The church is called to its witness by the living Christ (Luke 24:48; Acts 1:8, *inter alia*) and takes up the task of witness with joy in the midst of suffering (Acts 4:23-31; 5:40-42, *inter alia*). It cannot be stressed strongly enough that the church's responsibility is to give attention to the *urgency and quality of its witness.*

107. The church addresses God's call to people that they be converted from the reign of death and all its implications to the reign of life and all its implications. The reign of death has everything to do with human sin (cf. pars. 15, 87) because it enmeshes us in the violence of self-hating, self-justifying, self-protective, self-aggrandizing existence. It robs us of truth, hope and love. It makes us dangerous and destructive toward ourselves, each other, and our world. The reign of God, the reign of life, is the promise that death will not have the last word. The gift of God is life and freedom. The reign of life makes our self-protective attempts unnecessary as well as exposing them as impossible. But what is at stake in the church's call is *conversion,* nothing less! That is, a being transferred

from one reign to another (Col. 1:13). Jesus repeatedly describes the radical nature of the conversion in terms of not being able to serve two masters (Matt. 6:24), of building on rock or sand (Matt. 7:21-27), of following him instead of fulfilling filial obligations (Matt. 8:21-22), even of division in families and households (Matt. 10:34-39). It is a question of the object of one's final trust, one's ultimate concern.

108. Such radical conversion and transfer from one reign to another is inseparably connected in the church's life with the baptism it administers (cf. pars. 12-15). The church baptizes persons into the name of the God of the gospel (cf. Section 2), that is, into the reign of life. It baptizes persons into the community of the gospel (Section 3), that is, into the community that lives from and witnesses to the reign of life. It baptizes persons into the lifelong struggle to become and reflect in their lives what they are in fact by virtue of their baptism: the sons and daughters of God and the heirs of the promise of life (cf. pars. 114-123 below). All the baptized share in the eucharistic life and mission of the community of the reign of life. That is, witness to the reign of life is the calling of the baptized community as a whole as well as of each individual member in a manner appropriate to that member's age, experience, calling, and station in life.

109. The church needs to integrate sacramental life, ethics, and ecumenism into a unified understanding and practice of evangelization. Because our churches have a shared understanding of the meaning of baptism, because we recognize fully each other's baptisms, because we have similar rituals of baptism, and because we are striving to effect similar reforms in the administration of baptism, it is appropriate for our churches to give common attention to an understanding and practice of evangelization which has its focus in baptism. Indeed, in this

document we are attempting to bear witness to a shared understanding of the evangel not so that we may test or prove one another's orthodoxy, but rather so that the mission implications of the gospel (evangelization) may become part of our shared life and ministry.

110. We can here do little more than identify some components of an approach to evangelization when the church's baptism is its central focus. In theology and liturgy the church must be continuously attentive to the necessary connection between baptism and the content and character of the gospel: the eschatological reign of God has begun and is grounded in the life, death, and resurrection of Jesus of Nazareth. Therefore the call and witness of the church is: Be reconciled to God (2 Cor. 5:17-21), that is, be set free by the reign of life from the bondage of the reign of death.

111. The rite of baptism must reflect the radical character of justification by faith for the conversion taking place. The transfer from death to life is the "dying" to the reign of death and the being raised to the reign of life. Therefore our present baptismal rites require of candidates appropriate renunciations as well as affirmations. The Episcopal Church has canonical provision (*Book of Common Prayer,* p. 312) for renewal of the practice of administering baptism at select times during the Christian year: the Easter Vigil, Pentecost Day, All Saints' Day or Sunday, and the Baptism of Jesus (First Sunday After the Epiphany). The *Minister's Desk Edition* for the *Lutheran Book of Worship* (p. 30) calls for the same practice. The purposes of such reform and renewal include the use of such occasions for teaching about baptism, the appropriate involvement of the congregation in the baptismal rite, the reaffirmation of their baptism by the baptized, and the opportunity for disciplined preparation of candidates for baptism. While all baptisms can hardly be limited to a few occasions in the life of

the parish, the calendar focus for the administration of baptism should be the Easter vigil because it provides a thematic connection with the death and resurrection of Jesus and the candidate's being identified with that death and resurrection so that a death and resurrection of the candidate's own takes place.

112. The church has two components of its present baptismal practice which are in need of renewal and redefinition but which have significant potential for the church's mission of evangelization with a focus on baptism: the catechumenate and sponsorship for baptism. In most contemporary baptismal practice sponsorship is limited to the baptisms of infants and very small children. The role of sponsor is usually taken by family members or family friends. The new baptismal rites of our churches envision sponsors for *all* candidates. Further, the sponsor represents the church in bringing the candidate to baptism. These two factors provide openings for the church's ministry of evangelization. Whoever else functions at the actual baptismal rite, one or more sponsors from the congregation can have already been involved in the call and witness to the adult candidate, in involving the candidate in the catechumenate, in attending the candidate during the catechumenate, and in integrating the person newly baptized into the life and mission of the church. In the case of infants brought to baptism by a parent or parents who are already baptized members of the church, parents and family will be the primary sponsors. But even here they may be assisted by other members of the parish, and there may be a short period of instruction to prepare parents and family for their ministry in relation to a baptized infant. The catechumenate needs to be structured in such a way that it includes initiation into the life, teaching, rites, and ministries of the church with assistance from clergy, catechists, and other members of the church. Such a structured catechumenate would need to be extended over a period of months, not all of which would be spent in formal instruction. In all

of this it should be clear that baptismal sponsorship is the way the church *seeks* those who might not otherwise take the initiative, the way the church carries out God's mission of *sending* it into the world.

113. These reforms and approaches are necessary because the church, whether it thinks of itself in this way or not, is in fact in a missionary situation in Western countries no less than in the rest of the world. The massive increases in church membership which occurred in the United States between 1950 and 1970 did not necessarily mean that *conversions* to Christianity took place. Much of that increase in membership involved not a little identification of religion with American cultural values. The fact that areas of the United States with the largest population increase in the past decade (South and West) also have the lowest percentage of church membership is further indication that what happened after World War II was more a cultural trend than a period of Christian conversion. Hence we must be attentive both to the continued and even urgent *need* for evangelization and to the *quality* and faithfulness with which we engage in evangelization. These paragraphs are an attempt to identify the administration of baptism as an opportunity for our churches to develop a common and faithful approach to evangelization and conversion.

D. Mission and Ethics

114. The church's attention to ethics does not mean that it simply serves the public good by cultivating and encouraging behavior patterns characteristic of responsible citizenship. The Christian ethic does in fact ultimately serve the public good by encouraging honesty, stewardship, compassion, responsibility, education, and attention to peace and justice. But its focus is to ask how the good news of the reign of God in Jesus, the Christ, shapes the character and life of the people of God.

The teaching of Jesus and the apostolic exhortation are not intended to be an ethic for the state. They are intended to be part of the witness of the community that believes the gospel. (Cf. Matt. 5:3-16 and Romans 12–16 as two examples from the many that could be adduced.) What is at stake is the relationship of Christian ethics to the breaking in of the reign of God. The life of the people of God as a whole as well as the life of its individual members should reflect faith in the gospel.

115. Christians are not always agreed on concrete strategies for the church's life as witness to the reign of God. Deeply committed German Christians who were passionately opposed to the Nazi regime for reasons of faith and confession disagreed on whether or not to engage in violence against the Nazi regime, to cite but one paradigmatic example from our century. We cannot in this document begin to work toward agreement on concrete ethical implications of the gospel for our churches. We can, however, identify several dimensions of the church's ethical mission.

a. We affirm the necessary connection between the church's teaching of the gospel and administration of the sacraments on the one hand and its ethic on the other hand. While it is true that the church's gospel is the redeeming reign of God in Christ, not the church's life, nevertheless, the gospel has implications for the life of Christians which are inseparably linked to it (e.g., Matthew 5–7; Ephesians 4–6; Romans 12–16).

b. We affirm the necessity of common work on matters of life and the concrete issues of ethics. The magnitude and complexity of the church's attention to issues of peace and war, economic and social justice, compassion and stewardship, culture and life not only require resources for study which may be larger than our individual churches have available. Of equal importance is the fact that we need each other's perspectives.

c. We affirm and identify a list of areas which are in continued need of the church's faithful attention for study guidance for its members, and corporate as well as individual action where appropriate.

116. *Stewardship.* We have already indicated (pars. 79-81) that the Christian teaching on and confession of creation calls those who are grasped by the gospel to stewardship of the universe. Authentic stewardship involves something quite different from contributing to the support of the church, however important that is in itself. Stewardship begins with the offertory prayer with which we "set the table" at the Eucharist. The *Book of Common Prayer* suggests the bidding, "Let us with gladness present the offerings and oblations of our *life* and labor to the Lord" (p. 344). The *Lutheran Book of Worship* directs the congregation to pray: "Through your goodness you have blessed us with these gifts. With them we offer *ourselves* to your service and dedicate our lives to the care and redemption of all that you have made" (p. 68, italics added in both examples). All that we are and have is placed into the service of the reign of God. Our stewardship is nothing less than the concrete exercise of our partnership with the creator in the Christian vision of creation which is characteristic of the gospel. Therefore we need to be appropriately attentive to issues affecting the purity of air and water, management of the resources of water and soil particularly in relation to the use of chemical fertilizers, the cultivation of land only marginally suitable for growing crops, the poisoning or depletion of subsurface water, and many related concerns. We need to be concerned about our individual and corporate use of renewable and nonrenewable resources. We need attention to issues related to energy, to our care for the nonhuman creatures who inhabit the earth with us, and to the quality and care with which we move into the space beyond our planet.

Sexuality.

117. Stewardship in service of the Christian vision of creation involves us in the stewardship of our bodies and especially the sexual dimension of our bodily existence. Biologically we share many characteristics with animal existence. But our humanity means that we are capable of responsibilities and choices which transcend biology. Hence human sexuality is more than genital. It is a part of all human existence. It is a significant part of human decisions, human covenants, and human social order. The gospel provides us with a perspective which shapes our responsibilities and choices in the area of our sexuality.

118. We need attention to the interdependent roles of both celibacy and marriage as *vocations* for individuals in the people of God. We need continually to be recalled to chastity in both marriage and celibacy. We need to ask how the church witnesses to the reign of God in its teaching on celibacy and marriage. We need to ask how the church witnesses to the gospel when it encourages and seeks to minister to the lifelong commitment in marriage. We also need to ask how the church witnesses to the gospel when it engages in ministry to those in troubled marriages and to the divorced. We need attention to parenthood as a vocation in terms of the gospel and to the practice of birth control as a dimension of responsible parenthood.

119. *Homosexuality.*

a. In the context of a larger approach to the area of human sexuality and its relation to the reign of God we must be attentive to the issue of homosexuality. There are few areas of human existence in which the church stands in greater need of both wisdom and love. It would seem to some that the acceptance of homosexual behavior is inconsistent with significant portions of biblical testimony. It seems to others, however, that the Scriptures do not provide clear and consistent comment on homosexual relationships. Increasingly, therefore, Christians are finding it difficult to maintain a negative judgment over against all homosexual behavior, even though the search for a positive position remains equally elusive. A growing number of individuals in our churches raise the following questions not because there are ready answers but because the churches need to express compassion, discern righteousness, stimulate study, and urge the quest for a Christian perspective which can guide clergy and laity alike.

b. Is there any difference between the biblical context and our own which would require reconsideration of the church's traditional position on homosexuality? While the Christian doctrine of creation affirms life and procreation, does the same doctrine require us to affirm what may be involuntary differences in sexual orientation? Is there clear agreement among major authorities that differences in sexual orientation are in fact involuntary or irreversible? Can the condemnation which has frequently characterized the church's relationship to homosexual behavior be reconciled with the unconditional depth of divine grace and the universal breadth of divine love? Is there a faithful third alternative to celibacy and marriage? In view of the church's legitimate condemnation of all sexual promiscuity, which is basically predatory, can the church recognize somehow mutual care and commitment in a homosexual relationship as it does in heterosexual marriage? What insights from psychology, sociology, and anthropology can be helpful to the church in formulating an ethical vision for persons with a homosexual orientation? In its attempt to respond to these questions can the church listen faithfully, sensitively, and patiently in the light of Scripture both to the concerns and commitments of Christian persons with a homosexual orientation and to the whole range of concerns and commitments on the part of all of its members? Can the church be a place of genuine dialogue and reconciliation between individuals, families, and larger groups painfully affected by homosexuality?

c. The church needs to be attentive to this issue and to remind itself that no minority group, no matter how small, is beyond its mission and sensitive concern, that is, beyond the gracious and righteous will of God.

120. The church is required to think about how it engages in pastoral ministry with Christians who must face tragic circumstances which make painful choices necessary, who must deal with the competing claims of equally authentic values. The issue of abortion has evoked the concern of Christians on behalf of those women whose pregnancy is the result of victimization and oppression and on behalf of those parents who are faced with difficult choices when a continued pregnancy threatens the life or health of the mother or the viability and well being of the unborn fetus. Christians have been equally concerned about the fetus whose embryonic humanity has claims upon the compassionate care and protection of the larger society. This is especially true when abortion is used as a form of social engineering or birth control. Attention to the issue raises a number of attendant issues, including how public our instruction on the prevention of pregnancy ought to be, how available alternatives to abortion need to be, how our society ought to support single parents, especially the increasing number of early teen mothers, during the crucial early years of the lives of their children, how the church ought to teach and support the value of chastity in a culture saturated with encouragement of promiscuity, how the church ought to express its concern for the rights and responsibilities of women, and how the church ought to cultivate in the male partner a sense of responsibility for both chastity and paternity. The church's commitment to life, not death, requires it to ask both how life can be wanted and nurtured after birth as well as how it needs to be protected before birth.

121. *Compassion* and *Vocation.* Our churches have a long and

good tradition of engaging in ministries of compassion, attention to the needs of the sick, the suffering, the dying, the bereaved, and attention to providing relief and assistance for the victims of poverty, deprivation, and disaster. We have little or no difficulty making the connection between this humanitarian activity and the church's witness to the gospel. We need here to ask how we can engage in such compassionate witness together, as part of our growing together in shared life and ministry. We have similar common traditions in cultivating the concept of vocation, viewing the various aspects of our individual lives as callings from God, as ministries of God in and for the world. Indeed this is one of the more positive aspects of our Reformation heritage. We need to ask concretely about how the reign of God is related to vocation and ministry in the world.

122. *Social Justice.* Our churches have an ambiguous record with regard to involvement in issues relating to social justice. Indeed, one of the disagreements within our churches is whether or not the church as church ought to be involved in such issues. We wish to affirm questions of social justice as appropriate and in fact mandatory for the church's attention not because the church seeks to order the life of the state or because Christians have more practical wisdom available to them. Rather, the churches must address the questions of social justice because such questions are related to compassion and vocation and above all because such questions are related to the church's witness to the reign of God. That the community in immediate temporal proximity to the resurrection of Jesus saw a connection between the eschaton, the Eucharist, and the sharing of meals and property is evident from the early chapters of Acts, especially Acts 2:42-46 and Acts 5:1-11. The church's involvement in questions of social justice throughout its history has been expressed in its response to such issues as slavery, sexism, unequal education, racism and the exploitation of labor. The

question is not whether the church should be involved, but how. How does the corporate life of the church reflect its gospel, and how does the church serve as a community of guidance and support for its members as they exercise their vocations in the social and economic dimensions of society? In this context, American churches cannot evade the question of economic order. Are all economic systems morally neutral? Attention to such questions belongs to the inescapable implications of the gospel. The reign of God has special implications for cultivating equality of opportunity and education, for the overcoming of racism, sexism, ageism, classism, irrational fear of homosexual persons, totalitarianism, and any other oppressive and prejudicial manifestations of the reign of death. How does the church witness to an alternative future, the future of the reign of life? How does the church serve as the vehicle for the Holy Spirit, the Spirit of freedom and the openness of the future? These are the questions with which social ethics must wrestle.

123. *Peace.* The relationship of the gospel to the concern for peace is such a major theme of the Scriptures that it needs no documentation. The vision of the prophets that the messianic age would bring peace with it (e.g., Isa. 2:2-4; Micah 4:1-4) was echoed in the teaching of Jesus (e.g., Matt. 5:9-12, 38-48) and the apostles (e.g., Rom. 12:14-21; 1 Peter 2:18-25; 3:8-22). The questions arise because of the church's flawed and ambiguous witness in this implication of the gospel. We need to ask with urgency and clarity what our witness to the gospel means for Christian participation in the military services. It is not a foregone conclusion that Christians must abstain from military service. Both of our churches can draw on the "justifiable violence" or "just war" traditions as part of their heritage. The question is how these traditions can be clarified in terms of the practice of "total war" and the possession of nuclear weapons. We have the further task of schooling ourselves in our authentic traditions and of developing

institutional ways for raising the kind of questions which our traditions require. Since biblical *shalom* is more than the absence of war, we also need to ask how we can be peacemakers through attention to violence in our societies, to meaningful disarmament and the turning of our resources and energies toward peaceful purposes, to the economic needs of the world's poor, and to fostering relationships of understanding, exchange, and cooperation with our enemies, especially the Soviet Union and other Marxist-socialist societies. The basic concern is not how our churches support or change governmental policies, but rather how our own corporate life and the individual vocational ministry of our members witness to the reign of God, the triumph of life over death.

124. The magnitude and complexity of the agenda before us must not be a deterrent. God has given our churches many gifts and resources for attention to this agenda. Above all we must be open to and grateful for the resources of Christian churches other than our own. One of the fruits of ecumenical cooperation today is that we can listen to and learn from the documents, thinking, tradition, and life of churches as diverse as the Roman Catholic and the Mennonite. What must be the responsibility of our churches is the integration in the consciousness and life of all our members the dimensions of ecumenism, evangelization, and ethics as necessarily interdependent dimensions of the one mission of the church as it witnesses to the gospel of the reign of God.

Conclusion

125. We commend to our respective churches, their parishes, bishops, clergy and members, for study and action this common statement on the implications of the gospel.

126. We commend this document for study because in it we have sought to give common expression to our separate theological and ecclesiological traditions. We have attempted to utilize the eschatological horizon of the New Testament because this perspective has given the vision and hope of the gospel to Christian churches in a variety of contemporary contexts. We have selected from the richness of the New Testament witness the theme of the redeeming reign of God, a concept which the Gospels of Matthew, Mark, and Luke use to describe the mission and ministry of Jesus. We have spoken of the church as an eschatological community with a mission of witness to the redeeming reign of God. We have sought to provide an integrative focus for various facets of the church's life: its matrix in Israel and the implications this has for the church's commitment to Jews; its need for evangelical and catholic authenticity in worship, proclamation, and polity; its call to participate faithfully in God's mission for the world. We have sought to formulate a statement which will be both edifying and challenging.

127. We commend it for action because our work needs to be accepted or adopted by our respective churches as a further step toward full communion. Equally important are the specific recommendations for action which we have made in the areas

of worship, ecumenism, evangelism, and ethics. We call attention here to the paragraph locations and substance of those specific recommendations.

1. Paragraphs 29-31 take up the use of appropriate language for the address of God in prayer and worship, and we advocate the use of both masculine and feminine imagery in speaking about God.

2. Paragraph 42 builds on the identification of the church's matrix in Israel with recommendations for our contemporary relationship to Jews.

3. Paragraph 50 advocates the renewal of the Eucharistic liturgy in the parish through conscious movement toward celebration of the Eucharist every Sunday.

4. Paragraphs 100-104 contain recommendations for cooperative activity between Lutherans and Episcopalians in order to manifest the unity we have been given.

5. Paragraph 112 urges common work in evangelization organized around the administration of holy baptism.

6. Paragraphs 114-124 recommend common attention to the ethical dimensions of the Christian life in the areas of stewardship, sexuality, vocation, social justice, and peace.

None of the specific recommendations are dependent upon full communion. All are able to make our churches more faithful in their life and witness. If undertaken cooperatively, they can be a substantial vehicle for God's gift of unity to our churches.

128. We join our prayers with those of our Lord for faithfulness to the gospel and unity in our witness to it.

Notes

1. We have consistently used the phrase "reign of God" instead of "kingdom of God" except when quoting from the Revised Standard Version of the Bible.
2. Lutheran–Episcopal Dialogue II issued five "Joint Statements," the first of them being a "Joint Statement on Justification" (*The Report of the Lutheran–Episcopal Dialogue, Second Series, 1976–1980*, pp. 22-24). Paragraph "C" of the "Joint Statement" reads as follows:

   "In the Western Cultural setting in which our communions, Episcopal and Lutheran, find themselves, the gospel of justification continues to address the needs of human beings alienated from a holy and gracious God. Therefore, it is the task of the church to minister this gospel *with vivid and fresh proclamation* (italics added) and to utilize all available resources for the theological enrichment of this ministry."

   We affirm justification by faith alone and not by works in terms of an eschatological understanding of the gospel. The justification of the totality of our existence is disclosed only by the ultimate end *(telos)* of all history. We cannot justify ourselves by means of our efforts or achievements in any sphere because we cannot see, much less determine, the ultimate outcome of history. Indeed, our efforts to justify ourselves in the face of our rebellion against the call to love God and the neighbor are profound expressions of our sinfulness. The gospel is the proclamation that justification is the gift and promise of God. Jesus of Nazareth, crucified and raised from death for sinners, is both the ground and the hope of the ultimate outcome of history. The meaning of our cosmos and of ourselves is in him (Col. 1:13-20). He is the Alpha and Omega, the origin and the outcome. Trusting him as "righteousness" and "justification" means that we are free *for* our lives and our callings. We have no necessity to use them for justification. We are free to confess sins, to hear the truth of admonition, to experience the grace of God, because the meaningfulness and justification of our lives does not derive from our being in the right. The key term is "faith" because our justification derives from that event which is promise: Jesus' death and resurrection as God's judgment on our lives and as the outcome of all history.

3. Cf. Virginia Ramey Mollenkott, *The Divine Feminine* (New York: Cross-road Publishing Company, 1983), and Caroline Walker Bynum, *Jesus as Mother: Studies in the Spirituality of the High Middle Ages* (Berkeley: University of California Press, 1982).

4. "Israel's deed would be overcome, and the people's path to repentance would once again be open. Those who had ruined their lives through their hardening against Jesus receive from God, freely and without merit, the possibility of new life (in biblical terms, atonement). God transforms the murder of his emissary into a deed of his *faithfulness* to Israel (in biblical terms, covenant); he turns the death of his emissary, planned and brought about by men, into the establishment of *definitive and irrevocable* faithfulness to Israel (in biblical terms, new covenant) and thus preserves his claim on the chosen people of God." Gerhard Lohfink, *Jesus and Community* (Philadelphia: Fortress Press, 1984), p. 25.

5. Gustaf Aulen, *Eucharist and Sacrifice* (Philadelphia: Muhlenberg Press, 1958), p. 200.

6. *The Eucharist as Sacrifice,* Lutherans and Catholics in Dialogue III, pp. 187-198; *Eucharist and Ministry,* Lutherans and Catholics in Dialogue IV, pp. 7-33; *The Final Report,* Anglican–Roman Catholic International Commission, pp. 12-25; *Anglican–Lutheran Dialogue,* The Report of the European Commission, pp. 11-12 and 43-46; and *The Report of the Lutheran–Episcopal Dialogue,* Second Series, 1976-1980, (LED II), pp. 25-29.

7. Massey H. Shepherd Jr., "Ministry, Christian," *The Interpreter's Dictionary of the Bible,* Vol. III (Nashville: Abingdon, 1962), p. 386.

8. Leonhard Goppelt, *Apostolic and Post-apostolic Times* (London: Adam and Charles Black, 1970), p. 177.

9. "To serve means to demonstrate love to mankind out of a faith which forgoes the use of right and power and seeks God's help in Jesus. This love is to be demonstrated for the same purpose as it was by Jesus, to inspire a faith in God and compassion for others." Goppelt, *ibid.,* p. 178.

10. Jerome Quinn concludes his careful study of "Ministry in the New Testament" with the following summary:

    The structures of first century Ministry involved leadership both by groups (of two, three, seven, twelve, *apostoloi,* prophets, teachers, *episkopoi, diakonoi, presbyteroi*) and by single individuals even within the groups (Peter; Paul; James; Titus in Crete; Timothy in Ephesus; the *episkopos*). Though there was development in Ministry in the first century, it was not unilinear. It is historically more exact and eventually more instructive theologically to respect the differences in structuring the Ministry that existed simultaneously in different churches (Jerusalem, Corinth, Ephesus, Rome, etc.). (*Eucharist and Ministry,* Lutherans and Catholics in Dialogue IV, p. 100.)

11. Bernard P. Prusak, "Woman: Seductive Siren and Source of Sin?" *Religion and Sexism*, edited by Rosemary Radford Ruether (New York: Simon and Schuster, 1974), pp. 89-116.
12. Joachim Jeremias, *The Prayers of Jesus* (Philadelphia: Fortress Press, 1978), p. 94.

List of Participants

Episcopal Church, U.S.A.

The Rev. L. William Countryman
The Church Divinity School of the Pacific
Berkeley, California

The Rt. Rev. Mark Dyer
Bishop of Bethlehem
Bethlehem, Pennsylvania

The Rt. Rev. Richard F. Grein
Bishop of Kansas
Topeka, Kansas

The Rev. John R. Kevern, *secretary*
Assistant, St. James Cathedral
Chicago, Illinois

Dr. Marianne Micks (resigned, October 19, 1987)
Virginia Theological Seminary
Alexandria, Virginia

The Very Rev. William Petersen
Dean, Bexley Hall
Colgate-Rochester Divinity School
Rochester, New York

The Very Rev. John H. Rodgers, Jr.
Dean, Episcopal School for Ministry
Ambridge, Pennsylvania

The Rt. Rev. William G. Weinhauer, *co-chair*
Bishop of Western North Carolina
Black Mountain, North Carolina

Staff:
The Rev. William Norgren, The Ecumenical Officer
The Executive Council of the Episcopal Church
New York, New York

The Rev. J. Robert Wright
General Theological Seminary
New York, New York

The Evangelical Lutheran Church in America

The Rev. Paul S. Berge
Luther Northwestern Theological Seminary
St. Paul, Minnesota

The Rev. Walter R. Bouman
Trinity Lutheran Seminary
Columbus, Ohio

The Rev. Paul E. Erickson, *co-chair*
Bishop (retired), Illinois Synod of the L.C.A.
Chicago, Illinois

The Rev. Robert J. Goeser
Pacific Lutheran Theological Seminary
Berkeley, California

The Rev. William G. Rusch
Executive Director, Office for Ecumenical Affairs
Evangelical Lutheran Church in America
Chicago, Illinois

The Rev. Edward D. Schneider (formerly representative of the Division of Theological Studies, Lutheran Council in the U.S.A.)
Good Shepherd Lutheran Church
Champaign, Illinois

The Rev. Wayne E. Weissenbuehler
Bishop, Rocky Mountain Synod
Denver, Colorado

The Rev. Cyril M. Wismar, Sr.
Auxiliary Bishop (retired), East Coast Synod/A.E.L.C.
Falls Village, Connecticut

Staff:
The Rev. Joseph A. Burgess (until December 31, 1987)
Executive Director, Division of Theological Studies
Lutheran Council in the U.S.A.
New York, New York

The Rev. Daniel F. Martensen (beginning January 1, 1988)
Associate Director, Office for Ecumenical Affairs
The Evangelical Lutheran Church in America
Chicago, Illinois

The Lutheran Church–Missouri Synod

The Rev. Carl Bornmann
St. John's Lutheran Church
Luxemburg, Wisconsin

The Rev. Jerald Joersz, Assistant Executive Secretary
Commission on Theology and Church Relations
The Lutheran Church–Missouri Synod
St. Louis, Missouri

The Rev. Norman Nagel
Concordia Theological Seminary
St. Louis, Missouri

The text, *Implications of the Gospel,* was adopted on January 4, 1988, at Techny, Illinois, with affirmative votes by the following participants:

Episcopal Church, U.S.A.
The Rev. L. William Countryman
The Rt. Rev. Mark Dyer
The Rt. Rev. Richard F. Grein *(in absentia)*
The Rev. John R. Kevern, *secretary*
The Rev. Marianne Micks (resigned, Oct. 19, 1987) *(in absentia)*
The Very Rev. William Petersen
The Very Rev. John H. Rodgers, Jr.
The Rt. Rev. William G. Weinhauer, *co-chair*

Evangelical Lutheran Church in America:
The Rev. Paul S. Berge
The Rev. Walter R. Bouman
The Rev. Paul E. Erickson, *co-chair*
The Rev. Robert J. Goeser
The Rev. William G. Rusch
The Rev. Edward D. Schneider
The Rev. Wayne Weissenbuehler
The Rev. Cyril M. Wismar, Sr.

One negative vote was cast by the Rev. Carl Bornmann (see following statement).

Statement of the Representatives of the Lutheran Church–Missouri Synod

As this phase of the Lutheran–Episcopal Dialogue comes to an end, we the representatives of The Lutheran Church–Missouri Synod wish to express our gratitude for the privilege of full participation in the discussions of the dialogue. We are especially grateful for the opportunities which the dialogue has provided for joint study of the Word of God on theological issues addressed.

The Lutheran Church–Missouri Synod did not enter the Lutheran–Episcopal Agreement of 1982 which included the establishment of a "relationship of Interim Sharing of the Eucharist" and the authorization of a third series of dialogues to discuss outstanding questions to be resolved before full communion. Since this agreement was the basis for the preparation of the document on "Implications of the Gospel," two representatives of The Lutheran Church–Missouri Synod abstained from voting on the statement, and one representative voted no.

As members of the dialogue, the representatives of The Lutheran Church–Missouri Synod will forward the statement on "Implications of the Gospel" to the President of the Synod, with the recommendation that the Commission on Theology and Church Relations be asked to evaluate the statement and possibly to prepare a response.

LCMS Representatives to LED III
Carl Bornmann
Jerald Joersz
Norman Nagel

Study Guide

for

Implications of the Gospel

Introduction

The agreement on the *Implications of the Gospel,* which emerged from the third series of dialogues between Lutherans and Episcopalians, has the potential for bringing a greater vision of church to both traditions, and drawing them closer to their goal of full communion. Since those who facilitated this agreement had the freedom to focus on commonalities rather than differences in theological doctrine and the lifting of anathemas, the document includes, not only areas of agreement, but also concrete suggestions for the incorporation of these areas into the life of the churches. This study guide is designed to enable parishes and synods/dioceses to examine thoroughly the document and consider how they can most effectively take action on its implications. This study guide should provide a means to educate Lutherans and Episcopalians regarding the status of the theological dialogue between the two traditions and to challenge them to respond to the recommendations in the document. The sections which follow provide guidance for the leader and participants so that they can utilize the study guide most effectively.

Objectives: The suggested objectives for the entire course are as follows:

1. To define the gospel in terms of what God is doing in history.
2. To demonstrate that Episcopalians and Lutherans can speak with one voice about certain implications of the gospel.
3. To outline ways to communicate the gospel in a contemporary culture while remaining faithful to the biblical message.

Description of the sessions: The study guide includes five sessions with each following the theme of a major section in the document. It is suggested that the leader follow the sessions in order as they are designed to follow the schema of the document. Each session includes objectives, a summary of the material from the document on a theme, and questions for discussion. An optional devotional period focusing on the theme for the session could be included. The biblical passages in the text of the document could be used appropriately here. This might be supplemented by brief stories from the leader and/or participants to demonstrate a vivid expression of the gospel. Prayer and music on the theme, either of the entire course or that particular session, could lead effectively into a discussion of the topic.

Primary Resources:

1. *Implications of the Gospel.* Adopted at Techny, Illinois, January 4, 1988.
2. *The Lutheran–Episcopal Agreement: Commentary and Guidelines.* New York: Division for World Mission and Ecumenism, Lutheran Church in America, 1983.
3. *Lutheran–Episcopal Dialogue: Report and Recommendations.* Second Series, 1976-1980. Cincinnati, Ohio: Forward Movement Publications, 1980.
4. *Lutheran–Episcopal Dialogue: A Progress Report.* Cincinnati, Ohio: Forward Movement Publications, 1972.

Personnel: The study guide is written for use by clergy and/or lay group participants. It is aimed at small group adult study. Trained leaders should facilitate the study process, but where it is appropriate, leadership could eventually rotate among group members. The material can be easily adapted to the level and interest of the group. It may be helpful to openly acknowledge at the beginning that group members are at different points.

Settings: The material may be adapted to a variety of settings, but is highly appropriate for ecumenical dialogues or study groups with Lutherans and Episcopalians, both clergy and lay, at the parish and synod/diocese level. It could also be utilized at the regional level if provisions are made to facilitate small group discussion. Where ecumenical dialogue is possible, effort should be made to use that model so that the participants will have the opportunity to recreate the experiences of the members of the Lutheran–Episcopal Dialogue III. The guide can be used to facilitate discussions in Sunday church school classes or adult forums, Bible study groups, and retreats.

Time: The guide is written to provide for sessions of 45 minutes to an hour. The sessions may be extended through presentations by speakers with expertise on topics raised by the agreed statement or the dialogues in general (history, methodology, themes). If sessions are extended, allow for breaks for refreshments. If there is adequate time, special reports by participants may be added.

Session Plan: The session could begin with devotions including prayers, biblical texts, and hymns as noted above. In presenting the material, the leader should do the following:

• Create an atmosphere which fosters sharing and dialogue.
• Start with the experience of the participants, encouraging them to share their stories of the gospel.
• Make an effort to inform participants through a collegial model of learning.
• If a group is large, make a presentation in a plenary session with discussions following in small groups.

Dialogue Process: Dialogue will be crucial for a successful discussion of the document especially if the group includes both Lutherans and Episcopalians. Consider the following as means to facilitate dialogue:

1. Commitment—Be willing to prepare through careful study of the document and to engage in the process.
2. Commonality—Acknowledge the common belief in the priority of the gospel of Jesus Christ.
3. Conversion —Be open to change in one's views concerning one's own tradition, i.e., Lutheran or Episcopalian as well as the other tradition.

Session One: The Cross as Good News

Objectives:

1. To define eschatology in light of the articulation of the gospel in the New Testament.
2. To understand the significance of the reign of God as the word of the cross.
3. To identify the ways baptism makes the reign of God visible.

Section 1 of *Implications of the Gospel* deals with the grounding of the eschaton (outcome) of the gospel in the life, death, and resurrection of Jesus Christ. The starting point for the relationship of the eschatological dimensions of the gospel to Jesus Christ is Mark 1:15 which announces the inbreaking of the reign of God through the proclamation of Jesus. This announcement represents a fulfillment of the Old Testament prophecies and the consummation of the promises which they entail.

The New Testament uses vivid images to express the reality of the gospel. These expressions vary according to the writers and circumstances under which the text was written. This diversity of expression demonstrates the mystery of the power of the gospel, which in many ways defies concrete definition, but nonetheless cries for explication from those who have experienced its proclamation in their lives. Paul proclaimed the gospel in terms of "justification by faith in Christ." The Gospel of John describes the gospel in terms of "Word of God become flesh." The synoptic Gospels focus on the breaking in of God's reign through the life and ministry of Jesus. Mark, in particular, describes this as happening through the cross.

This cross, which is the good news in the New Testament, relates directly to the theological term *eschaton* which refers to the final outcome of history. The New Testament grounds this ultimate destiny for the world in the promise of God's final victory which has already begun through Jesus Christ and most especially through his death and resurrection.

The document highlights the significance of the resurrection of Jesus by focusing on the disciples' experience of it as related in the Gospel of Luke. A reading of Luke 24:21-31 reveals that the disciples had experienced a kind of conversion through their encounter of Jesus after his death whereby they saw Jesus as the epitome of the eschaton. Their original expectations of vindication of suffering outlined in the Old Testament had been shattered because the outcome of this encounter with Jesus was not only beyond their expectations, but it provided them with a taste of the promise of God's salvation. The implications of the gospel for the disciples were that the world had been made right, and the future promised an end to suffering for those who were followers of Jesus Christ. Examples of these convictions in the biblical texts are noted in the text of the document in paragraph 9.

In the encounter with the resurrected Jesus, the disciples understood the crucified one as the exalted one. They understood that even in the deepest humiliation, Jesus proclaimed the good news for the world. The resurrection signified that even death on the cross did not destroy God's promises for new creation and reconciliation for the world. God's hand in history meant that the reign of God would control the final outcome.

The church affirmed this "new creation" by embracing the relationship between creation and redemption and confessing the death and resurrection of Jesus. As a result of this, the church 1) acknowledged the Scriptures of Israel as canonical; 2) asserted that the God of creation is Jesus, his Father, and the Holy Spirit; 3) affirmed that the creature may be used by God to fulfill promises; and 4) confessed a belief in the resurrection of all because of Jesus. These became the testimony to the gospel as eschatological event which represented the fulfillment of promises and the hope of the world.

This eschatological event was signified by baptism into the death and resurrection of Jesus. Baptism was practiced by the early disciples who recognized that the reign of God is both present and future. According to the document this is expressed in two ways. First, baptism in the name of Jesus means both *initiation* into the community in which the eschaton is already present because of the death and resurrection of Jesus and *repentance* because of the ultimate realization of the promises of Jesus. Those who are baptized in the name of the triune God are recipients of God's grace and forgiveness of sins as promised in Col. 1:13-14.

Repentance and forgiveness may occur before baptism, but because of its indelible character as initiation into the death and resurrection of Jesus, something happens *to* the candidate. According to the document this is one of the primary reasons for baptizing infants. Since they share in the sinfulness of all humanity, they also have need of the promises of the reign of God described in the New Testament (e.g. Mark 10:14-16; Matt. 18:3). Repentance continues to be necessary for those who have been baptized inasmuch as the reign of God is not yet fully realized. According to the Scriptures, they are called to put off the old (their sinful nature) and put on whatever is characteristic of those who have been crucified and raised with Christ.

The second way that baptism signifies that the eschatological event is both present and future is that the Christian community continues to be plagued by all the temptations of the world even though the reign of God is experienced in the present. The initiation represented by baptism is one that plunges the recipient into conflict between the old age and the new. Martin Luther described this state of the baptized as *simul justus et peccator* or being righteous and at the same time remaining sinful. The document describes baptism as the sacrament *par excellence* of justification by *faith* because the baptized remain alienated from their creator but live with the present reality and future hope of the eschaton. A belief in justification by faith and not by works has been affirmed by Lutherans and Episcopalians in earlier dialogues. When seen in light of the eschaton, one of the implications of the gospel is that both churches must continue to proclaim justification by faith through baptism into the death and resurrection of Jesus Christ.

In the Lutheran rite of baptism and the Episcopal rite of baptism, the baptized are released from the bondage of sin and joined to the death and resurrection of Jesus. This promise given so vividly in the sacrament is linked to the renunciation of evil powers which would further alienate the world from its creator. Both Lutheran and Episcopalian liturgical traditions declare that the connection to the death and resurrection of Jesus calls the baptized to make an effort to wrest out sin and evil in themselves and in the world.

The next section of the document explicates the difficulty the baptized face in trying to destroy evil because of the bondage of sin. Although baptism signifies a release from the "old aeon" and its perversion of God's promises, the baptized remain under the power of sin and its allure. This may cause them to worship false idols and embrace power and self-preservation rather than struggle for peace and justice for all humanity. Such sin is exemplified by self-justification—a trust in one's own powers and achievements to the detriment of faith in God's mercy. For the baptized, bondage is destroyed through the reign of God but at the same time continues to pervade their lives and prevents them from succeeding in their efforts to destroy evil.

In light of the baptized remaining tortured by sin but at the same time being set free through the present reality of the message of the eschaton, the gospel is the "word and way of the cross." The resurrection is God's proclamation that Jesus has become the "Christ" by virtue of the cross. This "crucified one" is the definitive example for all humanity that God's reign destroys any attempts of the church to purport a theology of glory, and instead calls for a theology of the cross. The "word of the cross" is what the church uses to fight against any perversion of the gospel through political and military power.

The soteriological (saving, atoning) implications of the gospel are that through the cross of Jesus the reign of God is identified with the reign of one who suffers death for the sake of the world. This vision of the suffering servant, who redeems the world and becomes a victim to set the victimized free, begins with the story of the God of Israel and comes to fruition when the Messiah is proclaimed as the servant of God. As noted in the document, Mark 1:11 and its parallels may be connected with Psalm 2 and Isa. 42:1-4.

God's reign is described in numerous ways in the biblical texts, e.g., one who becomes a slave and dies a humiliating death (Phil. 2:5-11); one who is the "despised and crucified one" (1 Cor. 1:18—2:5) who is exalted through crucifixion (John 3:14). These and other images from the texts, which are noted in paragraph 18 in the document, proclaim the message that the cross of Jesus definitively establishes the reign of God. The gospel becomes the cross because it continues to struggle with all forms of evil and injustice which represent the "old aeon" to which all are bound through sin.

Questions for Discussion:

1. The New Testament uses a variety of images to describe the power

of the gospel. Examples from the document are the "reign of God" and the "word of the cross." Examine paragraph 18 for biblical references. How can we create images for the gospel that are appropriate in a contemporary culture and embrace the richness of the biblical witness? Use your imagination to recreate images of the gospel that describe your own experience of God's love and forgiveness. Do they transcend the ideologies of traditions, either Lutheran or Episcopalian? If they do, what does this suggest about the implications of the gospel?

2. In what ways does your parish or synod/diocese represent the "eschatological community"? Describe specific ways that you could make it more representative of a community in which the "good news of the cross" is proclaimed even in the presence of its sinful dimension. Use "visioning" to create pictures of what your community might be if you were to take action on those suggestions.

3. Examine the rite of baptism as found in *The Lutheran Book of Worship,* pp. 121-125 and in *The Book of Common Prayer,* pp. 301-308. How does each articulate the link between baptism and the death and resurrection of Jesus Christ? What implications does this have for worship and educational programs for Lutherans and Episcopalians? Examine paragraphs 12-15 in the document. Do the characteristics of baptism outlined in those sections parallel either and/or both baptismal rites noted above? If so, what words and phrases are used to describe those characteristics?

4. In paragraph 9 where the significance of the resurrection of Jesus is described, reference is made to Emmaus where Jesus encountered the disciples as the eschaton and broke the barriers of their limited expectations. Show how certain myths associated with each tradition, i.e., Lutheran and Episcopal, can be shattered to reveal the truth of the gospel. Begin by identifying the myths (stories about the other tradition which are not necessarily accurate) and then suggest specific ways to move beyond those to a greater understanding of the tradition not your own. Outline ways to take action on making changes in your parish or synod/diocese to accommodate these new learnings.

5. Give examples of phrases or slogans from the advertising media which are easily emptied of meaning but are effective in selling a product. Contrast those with the "reign of God" or the "eschaton"—phrases with many layers of meaning. What does this suggest about the power of language to proclaim the gospel? The writers of the document have intentionally used language other than the traditional theological terminology. What implications does this have for furthering the relationship between Lutherans and Episcopalians?

Session Two: The Story of the Gospel: The Death and Resurrection of Jesus

Objectives:

1. To demonstrate the importance of the historic character of the God of the gospel
2. To define the Trinity in terms of Father, Son, and Holy Spirit.
3. To identify ways of using both masculine and feminine imagery in speaking about God.

The doctrines of classical Christianity—the doctrine of Christ and the doctrine of the Trinity—are identified as doctrines of the gospel and discussed in Section 2. This section highlights the Christian understanding of God as *evangelical* (gospel-centered). In this context faith is equated with faith in the gospel of Jesus Christ.

The implications of the gospel lead to the confession of the church that the God of the gospel is the Father, Son, and Holy Spirit. The christological dogma is inextricably grounded in history—the history of Israel and the history of Jesus. It was through the history of Israel that the Scriptures emerged. These Scriptures tell the story of God's eternal relationship with a people who are called into a covenant with him who is their creator, redeemer, and sanctifier. Through this covenant God sends out prophets who find themselves called to alleviate suffering in the world while at the same time suffering themselves in order to work toward peace, justice, and wholeness for all creation.

Jesus of Nazareth was called into this story as an eschatological prophet with messianic claims. Through his crucifixion his enemies intended to reject all his words and claims to be calling Israel to proclaim the reign of God. The resurrection (Rom. 1:3-4 and Acts 2:36) declares that Jesus is the Christ and points the reign of God back to the cross. Through the encounters of the disciples with Jesus after the resurrection, came the realization that Jesus Christ was one with God and that the history of the life, death and resurrection of Jesus was the definitive expression of God's revelation.

The church's christological and trinitarian dogmas are bound to the historicity of Jesus Christ and the evangelical character of his proclamation. To understand the term *evangelical* is to recognize that the historical person Jesus through his crucifixion became the redeemer of the world. Through Jesus' death, God suffers, and through the resurrection, God's eschatological promises are fulfilled.

The document states three reasons why the thinking summarized above has implications for the gospel. First, the historical recovery of the truths of the gospel message do not necessarily make it easier to believe, but it confronts the emptiness of a trust in false gospels. The *historical character of the gospel* must be emphasized in order to be faithful to its message which has been preserved by the church in the "two natures" dogma of Chalcedon which witnesses to the reign of God through Jesus' death and resurrection.

Second, the story of the historical Jesus is the story of how the grace of God has become authentic in the world's history and God's history. Although the suffering God was known to Israel, the ultimate expression of God's grace is grounded in the death and resurrection of Jesus Christ. Through the cross, God has made a final and unconditional promise to the world—that death has been overcome, and the reign of God is present now and in the future.

Third, by viewing the cross as central in history, the authenticity of the gospel is preserved. The unconditionality of the cross, which attests to the proclamation of the historical Jesus who suffered in order to redeem the world, precludes any interpretation of the gospel which is triumphalistic and self-serving. The gospel of the church is grounded in the servanthood and ministry of Jesus.

The importance of the narrative of Jesus is evident in the discussion of the trinity and the gospel also. *Naming* is inherent in narrative so that to use "Father, Son, and Holy Spirit" to refer to the historical Jesus, is to ground the trinity in the story of God's promise to redeem the world. The triune God is the gospel which is proclaimed through the historical narrative of Jesus.

The centrality of the cross must be included in a discussion of the trinity because the narrative of the trinity is that both "Son" and the "Father" suffer on the cross. This is the focus of the love of the creator who is also redeemer, and is reflected in the "names" which attest to the present, but not yet fully realized, reign of God. The "naming" is highly significant because Jesus who is "Son" is sent by one whom he called "Abba," an intimate term for "Father." Jesus asked his disciples to use the name "Father" when praying for the eschaton.

This unity of the Son with the Father is illustrated most profoundly by the story of Jesus' death on the cross because it demonstrates how inextricably the two were connected. Biblical passages (Rom. 8:32; Mark 15:33-34; Gal. 3:13; John 3:16) are noted to indicate that on the cross both the Father and Son sacrificed for the redemption of the world. The soteriological reality is expressed in the narrative of God's giving his Son for us.

After having discussed the Father and Son, the document deals with the Holy Spirit, making reference to the farewell discourse of Jesus in the Gospel of John. In this book the Holy Spirit is the *paracletos*, the one who "stands alongside of" the persecuted community in the world. The Holy Spirit bears witness to the world concerning sin and righteousness and leads the community that is the bearer of God's revelation in Jesus Christ. The power of the Spirit is alive in the community and unites the Father and Son with both oppressors and the oppressed, participating in the suffering and overcoming the sin.

The document highlights that an understanding of the relationship between the proclamation of the suffering God and mission is crucial to the contemporary Church. To deny this is to forget post-Holocaust Europe or ignore the psychological suffering of middle-class America. The liberating message of the suffering God becomes an aid to mission because of its focus on God *Emmanu-el,* God with us, who brings hope, forgiveness, comfort, and resurrection. This message of God's holiness and uniqueness is expressed by Paul in Galatians where he speaks of the leading of the Spirit as death to old enslavements and life with the freedom of Christ to love one's neighbor (Gal. 5:1—6:6). The theme also occurs in the Ephesian letter where the Holy Spirit represents a down payment which guarantees our inheritance "until we acquire possession of it." The Holy Spirit, the *dynamis* of a new future, along with the Father and the Son, is the *Trinity,* the God of the gospel.

Paragraphs 29-31 speak to the concern about the overuse of the term "Father," particularly when God is addressed in prayer. These paragraphs challenge the churches to recognize that when Father is not used as part of the trinitarian name for God, it becomes a masculine image for God. The document calls the churches to advocate the use of feminine images of God as well as the traditional masculine imagery. The document does not suggest that the masculine imagery be dropped, but it asks that feminine images be included in an attempt to describe the fullness of God's glory. Two ways this can be done are to add feminine imagery in modifying clauses when addressing God (which has biblical foundations) and to introduce feminine symbols to describe the work of the Spirit.

The document notes that while some may substitute gender neutral terms such as "creator," "redeemer," and "sanctifier" for the trinitarian name, the churches should not simply substitute these terms because to do so is to suggest that function is identical with person. This is inaccurate because each of the functions applies to all three persons named in the trinitarian formulation.

The doctrine of the trinity must preserve the name "Father" because it is not just one biblical image among many. It is the name Jesus used to describe the one in whose history he participates, and it is part of the church's name for God—"Father, Son, Holy Spirit." To change the terminology by substituting another term for "Father" for the "Abba" of Jesus would be tantamount to destroying the liberating mission of the gospel.

The God of the gospel, as grounded in the history of Jesus Christ and confessed in the Trinity, is the God who is *one.* The trinitarian language is intended to capture the biblical message of the uniqueness of Jesus Christ in whom the fullness of God's revelation was given to the world.

Questions for Discussion:

1. Discuss the centrality of the cross and how it determines christological and trinitarian formulations. How can the concern for keeping the cross central unite Lutherans and Episcopalians?
2. The importance of the historic character of the gospel is discussed in this section and others. What are the implications of the shared belief in a gospel that is grounded in the history of Jesus Christ?
3. Paragraphs 29-31 advocate the use of both masculine and feminine imagery in speaking about God. Observe the ways God is described in your parish in your liturgies and educational materials. After having given careful attention to paragraphs 29-31, discuss whether feminine images of God are being used in the ways suggested in the document. How can Lutherans and Episcopalians cooperate in acting on the recommendations in the paragraphs cited?
4. Discuss the significance of preserving the "Father" image when describing the triune God. Why are names so important to an understanding of the Trinity?
5. Paragraph 29 cites biblical texts which include feminine images to describe God. Examine these carefully and discuss how Lutherans and Episcopalians might include them in a joint worship service. (Suggested resource: *Ecumenical Decade 1988-1989: Churches in Solidarity with Women—Prayer and Poems, Songs and Stories.* Geneva: WCC Publications, 1988.)

Session Three: The Church of the Gospel

Objectives:

1. To understand the relationship between the church as the eschatological community, the gospel, and the reign of God.

2. To recognize the continuity between Israel and the church.
3. To understand the three primary dimensions of the church's life: liturgy, polity, and doctrine.

Section 3 of *Implications of the Gospel* deals with the church as a necessary implication of the gospel. The document asserts that there is a necessary relationship between gospel and church which has to do with the eschatological reign of God. When Jesus ushered in that eschatological reign he called into being an eschatological community which was open to all people willing to be a renewed people of God; a community responsible for being the bearer of the gospel in history. This community, the church, is formed by the reign of God, its life is shaped by the gospel of the Christ as the crucified and resurrected one, and its message is an affirmation of the present and promised reign of God.

The document speaks of the continuity between the church and Israel: Israel is the church's matrix. Jesus' mission, his announcement of the presence of the reign of God, was to and through Israel. His commitment was to the renewal of Israel; a renewal of Israel's calling to be a "kingdom of priests and a holy nation" (Exod. 19:6). Jesus' death and resurrection did not signal the rejection of Israel. Rather, his death and resurrection signaled the inclusion of the Gentiles, with a renewed Israel, into that eschatological community. Even Jesus' calling of the 12 disciples was meant to demonstrate this continuity. Rather than forming a church distinct from Israel, the Twelve served in microcosm as symbols of a renewed Israel. The document stresses the point that the messianic vision of the people of God is to be "Israel plus Gentiles."

Three dimensions of the church's life are examined in this section: liturgy, polity and doctrine. Each of the dimensions is shaped by the community's identity as determined by the story (history) of the Scriptures with its climax in Jesus as the Christ. Each of the dimensions bears witness to God's reign. Each is a vehicle for communicating the identity and mission of the gospel. And each is dependent on the other two for a faithful witness of the church's calling.

Liturgy is the church's worship. Because etymologically liturgy means the work of the people, one's duties as a citizen, participation in the liturgy also involves ethics and mission. Worship is not divorced from the church's life and witness in the world.

Section 3 focuses attention on only one aspect of the church's liturgy: the Eucharist. The Eucharist "is the rite by which the church is identified as the eschatological people of God and which shapes the church's mission of witness to the breaking in of the reign of God." On the Lord's day the baptized gather as the eschatological community in thanksgiving for, and in remembrance of, the life, death, and resurrection of Jesus Christ, to share that meal instituted by our Lord on the night before his death. Through the Eucharist those who are baptized receive the promise that they are the community of God's reign and receive the invitation to share in the mission of Christ. In the Eucharist the church receives and renews both its identity and the shape of its mission; the church is "identified by the body of Christ" and is "called to be the body of Christ." For this reason the Eucharist assumes special significance in the life of the church.

Lutherans and Episcopalians have placed different emphases on their understanding of the Eucharist. Lutherans have emphasized that Christ is present in the Eucharist as the once-for-all sacrifice for the forgiveness of sins and that his presence is not contingent upon the faith of the participants. Faith receives, rather than effects, the promise of Christ. Episcopalians have emphasized that the Eucharist is the church's sacrifice of praise and thanksgiving, the way by which Christ's sacrifice is made present and by which he unites the community to the offering of himself. Though the emphases have been disparate, members of the dialogue have been able to affirm both emphases as faithful expressions of the Eucharist.

The church's polity is the second dimension of the church's life discussed in this section. Polity is to be more widely understood than in terms of governance and ordering of ministries, though it certainly involves both. The document defines polity as "the way the church as the body of Christ under historical conditions is freed by the gospel to live together so that the patterns and powers of its life reflect and witness to the reign of God. . . ." Polity is at the heart of the church's life together as an eschatological community; it shapes the community's corporate life in terms of discipleship.

Two primary characteristics of the community's corporate life are represented by the words "to send" and "to serve." The church is sent as Christ was sent into the world; the church is an apostolic community. The church is also called to a life of service to Christ and to one another; the church is a diaconal community. There is considerable diversity in the expressions of the church's apostolic and diaconal ministry, as there was in the life of the early church. Polity facilitates in maintaining the unity of faith within the context of diversity.

The document assumes that the church and its polity are subject to renewal and reform and identifies two norms for the renewal of the church's polity: collegiality and subsidiarity. Collegiality involves shared responsibility for leadership at all levels of the church's life. It is meant to guard the unity of the church while preventing a centralized authority from assuming all responsibility for leadership. Subsidiarity is closely related to collegiality. Subsidiarity assumes that every member of the community should participate in decision making and leadership and that whenever possible decisions should be made by other than the primary church leaders. Subsidiarity assumes that the minority viewpoints within the community must be protected and listened to. Since polity includes governance, order, and authority, the principles of collegiality and subsidiarity prevent that governance from becoming too centralized and from excluding the participation of the faithful in ordering the life of the eschatological community.

The church needs always to be careful to allow the power of the Gospel to transform, reform, and renew its life and its polity. Neither the church nor its polity are static. The responsibility of the faithful is to be responsive to the gospel's power and to discern which reforms are both necessary and able to maintain the integrity of the church's life, witness, and tradition. The ordination of women is cited as such a necessary reform of the church's polity. Though there is disagreement between and within the churches about the fidelity of this particular reform to the church's tradition there can be no disagreement that the issues involved which must be addressed are crystal clear. It is the church's responsibility to determine parameters within which reform is admissible.

The greatest differences between Lutherans and Episcopalians exist at the level of church polity. One of the major obstacles to full communion between these churches is their understanding of the function of bishops and of the historic episcopate. The churches have not yet reached complete agreement on this aspect of polity, but members of the dialogue have agreed on the ways in which polity serves the life and witness of the church.

The third dimension of the church's life is doctrine, which is defined as authentic Christian teaching. The document affirms the necessity for normative doctrine which serves to evaluate the quality and consequence of the church's proclamation. Doctrine helps to maintain the unity of the faith by safeguarding the fidelity of the proclamation of the gospel. Proclamation of the gospel is rooted in the Holy Scriptures; it is the canon of Scriptures which provides access to the authentic gospel. But the proclamation is not simply a reiteration of those Scriptures—it is a living proclamation that requires interpretation and which emerges from the life of the community. Doctrine provides the requisite interpretive tools. It also sets parameters beyond which the church's teaching must not extend and still be gospel while at the same time identifying what *must* be said if the gospel is to continue to be claimed.

Doctrine has functioned differently for Lutherans and Episcopalians, but both have means whereby their proclamation and teaching are measured. For Lutherans, doctrine has largely functioned prescriptively: there has been considerable doctrinal and theological homogeneity which emphasizes what Christians *ought* to teach. Fidelity to doctrine is measured by the standard of documents in the 1580 *Book of Concord,* especially the catholic creeds, the Augsburg Confession and the Small Catechism. For Episcopalians, doctrine has largely functioned descriptively: there has been theological and doctrinal variety which emphasizes what Christians, in fact, teach. Fidelity to doctrine is measured by the *Book of Common Prayer.*

The chapter concludes with the important reminder that the church and the reign of God are distinct: the reign of God is the church's source to which the church is called to bear witness.

Questions for Discussion:

1. What is meant by the assertion that the church is the principal implication of the gospel in human history?
2. Paragraph 42 suggests that the messianic vision of the people of God includes "Israel plus Gentiles" and that this vision has implications for Christian-Jewish relations. Read Romans 9–11 and discuss the issues of God's continuing relationship with the Jews, particularly the two questions of whether or not God has abandoned the Jews and whether or not God's covenant with Israel has been superseded by the new covenant. What are the implications of this discussion for evangelization? How might Lutheran and Episcopal churches work together to further overcome the centuries of oppression and persecution which have poisoned the relationship between church and synagogue? Where do you see examples of church and synagogue witnessing together "to humanity's flawed and broken capacity to be the bearer of the messianic vision"?
3. Paragraph 50 asserts that the weekly and festival celebration of the Eucharist is a significant implication of the gospel. In your parish, is the Eucharist celebrated every Sunday as "the principal act of Christian worship"? If not, where are the points of resistance which prevent movement towards this goal? In what ways does the weekly celebration of the Eucharist sharpen the church's focus on its life and mission? What relationship does recovery of the liturgy have to newly empowering the whole people of God?
4. Paragraph 51 says that the most obvious obstacle to full communion between Lutherans and Episcopalians is church polity, particularly the two churches' different understandings of the function of bishops and the historic episcopate. Discuss these differences of understanding: how do Lutherans and Episcopalians understand the nature and function of the episcopate? Why is this difference in understanding an obstacle to full communion?

5. Paragraph 57 identifies the church's "freedom for reform" as a demonstration of the power of the gospel and cites the ordination of women by the churches as a specific example of a recently undertaken reform. How is the church to determine when such reform is faithful to the gospel and coherent with tradition? How might the episcopate be similarly reformed by the churches?
6. Paragraph 69 poses two questions about use of the Lutheran *Book of Concord* and the Episcopal *Book of Common Prayer.* Discuss the question appropriate to your tradition. "How, if at all, does the *Book of Concord* shape the worship, including administration of the sacraments, in Lutheran parishes? How, if at all, does the *Book of Common Prayer* shape proclamation and teaching in Episcopal parishes?"

Session Four: The World and the Gospel

Objectives:

1. To define *world* theologically, within the framework of the proclamation of the gospel.
2. To understand the relationship between the doctrine of creation and the problem of human sin.
3. To understand the relationship between the world and God's future reign.

Section 4 of *Implications of the Gospel* discusses the relationship between the world and the gospel. The world is defined both as the context within which the church exists and as that which is created by God. This dual emphasis prevents a definition of *world* which is primarily negative, which views the world as necessarily hostile to the gospel and to the eschatological community. Rather, the world is viewed theologically as God's creation, the context in which the church resides and to which the gospel must be addressed.

The document acknowledges the difficulty of defining the term *world* because it has a variety of meanings in the New Testament and in contemporary society. In the New Testament the term describes that which is hostile to Christ *and* that which is the object of God's love. In contemporary definitions it is sometimes synonymous with the universe and at other times it refers to a cultural context.

The major issue at stake in any theological discussion of the world is that of the proclamation of the gospel. Religious language has been rendered nearly meaningless in the public sphere because of post-Enlightenment secularity. The result has been a shift from the public to the private sector; religion has become privatized. The privatization of religion, however, is antithetical to the gospel and the nature of the community called into being by the reign of God. The privatization of religion "thus challenges the church's very ability to address the world meaningfully with a public word."

Another challenge posed by the contemporary world to the churches comes from the world's great non-Christian religions which have doubled in size in the past 50 years. Christianity has grown, but not by the same proportions. Christians have been forced to rethink their pre-World War I and II strategy of service and evangelism as opportunities for either have been curtailed in some parts of the world. Western Christians, in particular, face the question of how to proclaim the gospel in either a secular or a non-Christian religious world. Obviously the three renewal movements mentioned in the document (evangelicalism, fundamentalism, and the charismatic movement) reflect efforts by Christians to proclaim the good news of God's reign to the world, even though the consequences have been negative as well as positive.

The document addresses the problems of evil and human sin within the context of the doctrine of creation, which is grounded in the gospel. The people of God affirm that God created the world and in so doing he brought order out of chaos, light out of darkness, life out of death. Christians confess Jesus to be the one through whom all things were made. Creation reflects God's intention and God's love; it is good and vital.

Creation is also marred by evil and human sin which need to be addressed by the gospel. The gospel makes three primary assertions in the face of evil: God accepts the consequences of having created a world in which there is freedom to choose life or death; God suffers because of and on behalf of his creation; and the cross is the way God's love and life triumphs over evil and death.

Because of sin humanity is alienated from God's reign and from God's intention for his creation. Sin, according to the document, is more appropriately defined as misbelief than misbehavior. Misbelief, or sin, trusts things and people other than or more than God. Misbelief refuses to see God's presence and reign in the world. The gospel addresses sin with the good news that it is forgivable and that God loves the world no less because it is marred by misbelief and disobedience. God's people are given the grace to see the world from the perspective of the gospel, to be able to confess to God that which God knows and says to us. The cross is the way God has chosen to heal creation, to forgive sin, and to restore that relationship which is severed by sin.

The gospel also offers a new vision for the world's future. The world and the kingdom or reign of God are no more synonymous than are the church and the reign of God. God's future reign is present and visible in the world but it also transcends the world. The people of God cannot hurry God's final and triumphant reign by patching up creation to resemble that which is anticipated. The gospel message promises that God's reign has and will triumph over sin and death and the creation waits in eager expectation for that final triumph.

Questions for Discussion:

1. Paragraph 71 suggests that the form of secularity which must be of particular concern to Western Christians is the way in which it has called into question the public meaningfulness of religious language. Discuss the significance of this for Lutherans and Episcopalians. Can the public meaningfulness of religious language be restored? If so, how? If not, why not? What are the consequences of each?

2. What account would you give for the statistics from the *World Christian Encyclopedia* indicating that the great non-Christian world religions have doubled in size and maintained their proportion of the world's population while Christianity has increased

by only 50% and decreased its proportion of the population? How can the gospel "be addressed to a postcolonial world, and in the midst of resurgent, vital world religions" (par. 74)?

3. Discuss why the Christian doctrine of creation is a major implication of the gospel.
4. In light of the doctrine of creation, how are we to understand the existence of evil in the world?
5. Discuss the definition of sin (par. 87) as misbelief rather than misbehavior. Identify the foci of your faith and trust when not directed towards God's redeeming reign.
6. How are we to understand God's judgment as a sign of God's care for the world?

Session Five: The Mission of the Gospel

Objectives:

1. To recognize the centrality of prayer to participation in Christ's mission.
2. To understand the interdependence of ecumenism, evangelism, and ethics.
3. To explore specific ways in which the Lutheran and Episcopal churches can given common attention to mission.

Section 5 of *Implications of the Gospel* concludes that mission is the implication of the gospel *par excellence*. To believe in, confess and follow Jesus as the Christ necessarily involves Christians in their Lord's mission, the mission of the reign of God. The document suggests that this engagement in Christ's mission has as its focus the Lord's Prayer: to pray in Jesus' name means to be identified with and shaped by his mission, ministry, and promises. The Lord's Prayer marked Jesus' disciples as his own while at the same time it provided a succinct summary of Jesus' proclamation of the reign of God. Jesus identified the relationship between his followers and God in the same way he was related to God: as children to their "Abba." The petitions asking that God's name be made holy and that his kingdom come are prayers of messianic hope and promise. The disciples recognize that what is true "in heaven" is realized "on earth." The petitions regarding food and forgiveness also reflect messianic hope and promise: there is hope for the messianic banquet and the eventual forgiveness of sins while at the same time there is recognition of the need for "daily bread" and trust that we need not wait for the final judgment for sins to be forgiven. And finally, Jesus teaches his disciples to pray that they not be put to the test but delivered from the evil which inevitably assaults those who participate in the mission and reign of God.

Prayer is not isolated from participation in Christ's mission: it is rather the foundation upon which the life of the community must be built. The document emphasizes this connection between prayer and mission when it says, ". . . if our prayers are shaped by the Lord's Prayer, in the end we will be taken up into the ministry and mission of the reign of God. . . . In prayer we offer ourselves and seek to discover how and in what concrete form we will be taken up into the mission of the reign of God. . . ."

Worship is the context within which prayer is set because it is within this context of word and sacrament that the people of God receive their identity and mission, the gift of Christ and the vocation of witness. The document organizes concrete dimensions of the church's mission and witness around three mutually interdependent themes: ecumenism, evangelism, and ethics. In pursuing its mission, the church must give equal attention to ecumenism, evangelism, and ethics, and must recognize their dependence upon one another.

Ecumenism is the means whereby Christians seek to "discover how the unity they have already been given by the gospel can be manifested faithfully in terms of the church's mission." The manifestation of the church's visible unity is the people of God's fundamental vocation as they participate in Christ's mission and witness. The world can only see, know and believe what God has done in Jesus Christ to the degree that the Christian community reflects that messianic mission in its life and work and by its unity. The document lists examples of specific actions the Lutheran and Episcopal churches can engage in together, specifically in the areas of education, leadership, liturgy, and ecumenical strategy. The examples given are by no means exhaustive, but are meant to encourage the two churches to take as many steps together as possible on the road to full communion. Full communion is not prerequisite to any of the suggested steps.

Evangelism is the church's witness to the good news of the reign of God through its words, worship, and deeds. It is the "church's responsibility to give attention to the *urgency and quality of its witness.*" The goal of this witness, of evangelization, is radical conversion: the transfer from the reign of death to the reign of life, the reign of God. This conversion is inseparably connected in the church's life with baptism, for it is by being baptized with water in the name of the Father, Son, and Holy Spirit that the people of God enter this new life and share in the eucharistic life and mission of the baptized community.

The Lutheran and Episcopal churches are encouraged to give common attention to an understanding and practice of evangelization which is focused in baptism. The document identifies some components of such an approach to evangelization: an awareness of the connection between baptism and the content and character of the gospel; a rite of baptism which reflects the radical character of justification by faith; and the renewal and redefinition of the catechumenate and sponsorship for baptism. The administration of baptism may be an opportunity for the churches to develop a common approach to evangelization which is attentive to the need for evangelization and to the quality and faithfulness of our efforts.

The third theme, that of ethics, focuses on the question of how the good news of the reign of God in Jesus Christ "shapes the character and life of the people of God." The issue of ethics is a question of how the life of the Christian community reflects the reality of the reign of God.

Recognizing that there is often disagreement about specific ethical stances and strategies, the document identifies several dimensions of the church's ethical mission which can serve as common ground: the necessary connection between the church's teaching of the gospel, administration of the sacraments, and its ethics; the necessity of common work on matters of life and the concrete issues of ethics; and identification of those areas in continued need of the church's attention for study, guidance for its members, and action where appropriate. These areas of study and attention include stewardship, sexuality, compassion and vocation, social justice, and peace.

Although the ethical agenda for the churches is complex, the churches must recognize those gifts and resources given by God which enable mutual participation in the mission of the reign of God.

Implications of the Gospel concludes with a commendation to the two churches for study and action and calls attention to several specific recommendations which if undertaken cooperatively, can be a "vehicle for God's gift of unity to our churches."

Questions for Discussion:

1. Study the Lord's Prayer (Matt. 6:9-13; Luke 11:2-4) and discuss the implications of the prayer for the church's mission and ministry.
2. Paragraph 98 suggests that the fundamental vocation of the people of God is to manifest visible unity. Identify where you see that unity most visibly manifested in the life of your parish, diocese, or synod.
3. Paragraph 100 lists specific examples of ways in which the Episcopal Church and the Evangelical Lutheran Church in America might engage in common education and shared leadership. Discuss the feasibility of each of the examples. What additional examples do you think of, particularly which might be initiated by your parish or diocese or synod? What are Episcopalians and Lutherans already doing together in your area? What more would you like to see happen and how can you facilitate that?
4. Paragraph 112 identifies two components of the church's baptismal practice in need of renewal and redefinition, which have significant potential for evangelization: the catechumenate and sponsorship for baptism. Discuss the current practice of your church with respect to these two components. How would their renewal and redefinition affect evangelization? How might you initiate necessary changes in either or both of them?

5. Paragraphs 115-124 identify several dimensions of the church's ethical mission which require the churches' common attention. Which of these dimensions is your church paying particular attention to? Which are being worked on ecumenically? How might Lutheran and Episcopal churches most effectively engage together in the church's ethical mission?

6. Paragraph 124 says that the churches are responsible for the "integration in the consciousness and life of all our members, the dimensions of ecumenism, evangelization, and ethics as necessarily interdependent dimensions of the one mission of the church as it witnesses to the gospel of the reign of God." Discuss ways in which the churches can best assume that responsibility. What resources are necessary? Which are available and which are lacking?